LEADING CHAOS:
AN ESSENTIAL GUIDE TO MANAGING CONFLICT

LEADING CHAOS

AN ESSENTIAL GUIDE TO
CONFLICT MANAGEMENT

ALEXANDRIA A. WINDCALLER

International Standard Book Number (ISBN): 1-884540-59-7

Haley's
P O Box 248
488 South Main Street
Athol, MA 01331
1.800.215.8805

Book designed by Marcia Gagliardi and Alexandria A. Windcaller.
Cover designed by Elizabeth Yoakum.
Photography by Tom Hurlburt.
Edited by Marcia Gagliardi and Jane Gagliardi.
Printed by The Highland Press.

Library of Congress Cataloguing in Publishing data:

For Carlen

Goal-Oriented Intervention Approach
CRISIS PREVENTION GOAL
PERSONAL SAFETY GOAL
SCENE SAFETY GOAL
CONFLICT MANAGEMENT GOAL
PHYSICAL MANAGEMENT GOAL

Ten Tips for Re-Directing Conflict
1. Say a Lot by Saying a Little
2. Remember that Silence Works
3. Acknowledge Emotions
4. Take Things One Step at a Time
5. Set the Pace
6. Be Mindful of Words that Escalate
7. Actively Listen
8. Avoid Objectifying Yourself
9. Tell It Like It Is
10. Create Opportunities

The Response Goal-Oriented Intervention Model is developed by
Alexandria A. Windcaller
Post Office Box 191
Wendell, Massachusetts 01379
www.responsetrainings.com
info@responsetrainings.com

Goal-Oriented Intervention Model

CRISIS PREVENTION   →   *Prevent Conflicts from Occurring*
GOAL

by

Identifying Potentially Dangerous Indicators
Feel, Look, Listen Approach

↓

Drop the Content

↓

Create an Action Plan

Conflict

↓

"Am I Safe?"
Pause
Exhale

↓

PERSONAL SAFETY   →   *Make Myself Safe*
GOAL

by

Regaining Self-control
Calling for Back-Up
Having Someone Else Intervene
Not Intervening

↓

"Is the scene safe?"
Feel
Look
Listen

↓

SCENE SAFETY   →   *Make the Scene Safe*
GOAL

by

Separating Conflicting Parties
Removing Physical Objects
Containing an Angry Person
Moving Away from Spectators
Creating an Alliance

↓

CONFLICT MANAGEMENT   →   *Help Those in Conflict Regain*
GOAL   *a Sense of Self-control*

↓

PHYSICAL MANAGEMENT   →   *Cause No Harm*
GOAL

Contents

Illustrations

Goal-Oriented Intervention Approach chart
segments accompany text appearing on
Pages 11, 31, 39, 43, 48, 55, 77, 78, 96, and 125.

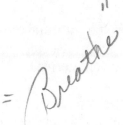

= "Breathe"

Introduction

Chaos reigns in a climate of confusion. The methodical attacks executed September 11, 2001, against the United States at the World Trade Center and the Pentagon created a momentary sense of disorder throughout the world.

Yet as quickly as chaos can overwhelm, it can just as quickly be squelched. At the WTC twin towers, moments after the first plane crashed, some of the trapped workers on the top sent out e-mails to family members and loved ones to say good-bye. Those inside the building who were able to walk down the stairwells did so in a calm fashion. Perhaps the air of calm stemmed from the words of fire-fighters as they hurried upwards past the mass of people coming down the steps. "Breathe" was a key word spoken by rescue workers to those in flight. In spite of the intensity of the disaster on the streets of New York and at what is now referred to as Ground Zero in downtown Manhattan, chaos was quickly managed.

Once people are able to get their bearings in the sea of confusion, order prevails. Some people have natural leadership skills, enabling them to see through the chaos of the moment. Not all people stabilize themselves at the same rate during a tumultuous scene. Many people rely on others who have the wherewithal to stay on course or seek professionals trained to perform specific crisis intervention tasks. At the crash scenes of September 11th the specialist were fire-fighters, police officers, paramedics, hospital staff, and construction crews. Many who had the capacity to seek order even as chaos unfolded in front of them volunteered to help at the attack scenes.

After chaos reigned briefly on September 11, 2001, order prevailed. Although many people may never experience complete resolution or closure following the terrorist acts, we all witnessed acts of goodness that will help provide us with enough resolve to move forward with our lives.

The goal of *Leading Chaos: An Essential Guide to Conflict Management* is to provide a safety-based goal-oriented model that professionals and non professionals alike can use to help bring order to minor conflicts like a family quarrel to physical confrontations like a fist fight.

Terrorism wages attacks against the psyche. The chaos that follows after a biomedical terrorist act or bombing can be managed by skilled workers and ordinary citizens who choose to lead chaos. Now more than ever we see the need to cultivate the skill of managing conflict—generating order from chaos.

managing conflict
* — generating order from chaos.

Simplify Conflict

You gain strength, courage, and confidence by every experience in which you really stop to look fear in the face. You must do the thing you think you cannot do.
—Eleanor Roosevelt

I am a reluctant authority in the field of conflict management. It is not that I shy away from conflict, especially after some sixteen years of teaching crisis intervention skills. I just can't heartily say that I chose this endeavor. Fate has played an important role in my life.

The first conflict management program I took part in was at Long Lane School in Middletown, Connecticut, a minimum and maximum security facility for adolescents. I worked there as an outdoor educator in the Youth Challenge program. Long Lane School is a correctional program for males and females between the ages of eleven and eighteen. All of the residents are sent there by the court system for crimes ranging from minor misdemeanors to murder.

I managed an on-site rope course and facilitated team building programs for the residents. During the summer, I worked with a co-instructor taking the teens on canoe trips down the Connecticut River and on overnight backpacking trips to the Appalachian Trail in northwest Connecticut. Working so closely with young criminals dictated the need to seriously hone my skills in conflict management.

A year after beginning this job, I was asked to participate in a new program being introduced at Long Lane called The Humane Process of Defense and Control. This was a crisis intervention program for staff who managed potentially volatile clients and was based on the federal corrections model that emphasized physical management of volatile behavior. My former supervisor was less than pleased when she found out that I had signed on while she was out on vacation. I was to become an instructor, and teaching courses was going to take a big chunk of my time. The administrators of our facility, however, were genuinely pleased to have a woman participating in the all-male instructor training program. Having a woman as a lead instructor complemented Long Lane's unwritten policy that all staff regardless of gender could physically intervene and manage a crisis.

It quickly became apparent, however, that the program was one-sided and dangerous, with an emphasis on the physical and a lack of emphasis on verbal de-escalation. The physical techniques used a form of pain compliance to coerce a person to submit. Without a more balanced approach toward conflict management that integrated verbal intervention and safe physical management techniques, the program was destined to fail. Besides, I wasn't interested in a career in corrections. Soon, I was ready to move on. I quit my job and began designing outdoor gear under my own label. I looked forward to a life far away from locked doors and angry people. Fate, though, had other plans.

Within a year of pursuing my new enterprise, I was asked to work as a consultant to the State of Connecticut. The Department of Children and Families needed help integrating the Humane Defense program into five additional facilities. These sites included acute psychiatric hospitals and residential treatment centers. Even though I disagreed with the philosophy, I signed on to what I thought would only be a temporary position.

*verbal vs physical

I began researching alternative methods of conflict management and envisioned a program emphasizing verbal de-escalation skills. Humane Defense used physical management techniques derived from Aikido. I knew that in order to speak with any authority on the topic of conflict-crisis intervention, I needed both verbal and physical expertise. It was a natural choice for me to simultaneously begin training in the Japanese martial art of Aikido while developing a more holistic conflict ③ management approach.

Aikido does not use strikes or kicks to subdue an attacker. Aikidoists learn to blend with an attack. For instance, instead of blocking a punch, requiring a great deal of physical strength, you allow the hit to go through. This means if you are on the receiving end of the punch, you have to learn how to step off to the side of the strike. The person delivering the punch will typically throw full weight behind the hit, falling off balance. When a person is just off center, leaning too far forward after his punch, he can be easily moved without the need of brute force.

turn a walk i walk i person

turn away

Verbal arguments are, metaphorically speaking, the same as physically blocking a punch. Loud and forceful arguments usually end with only one victor. Blocking another person, whether physically or verbally, sets up the same combative dynamic. Instead of blocking another person's viewpoint, you could figuratively step to the side of a disagreement, just as when stepping off the line of a strike, as in Aikido. Practicing a non-reactive approach toward conflict keeps you out of harm's way by reducing your chances of becoming the target of another person's anger. Such a vantage point provides breathing room for both parties to seek nonviolent alternatives for working through a dispute.

verbal or physical

step aside

In Aikido, the goal is to lead disputes toward safe conclusion and not to annihilate an attacker. I interpret the philosophy of this art as learning to see the higher self in even the angriest person. The higher self is that person within each of us who can listen to reason, wants merely to be seen, not judged, and wants to feel safe. Speaking to an attacker's higher self creates an opportunity to avoid violence. It is a simple gesture, yet it is a novel technique. It takes people by surprise when you don't meet a violent interaction by becoming violent yourself.

Aikido is very aerobic. Over the course of an hour-long practice, you may roll forward or fall backward over a hundred times. Learning to fall safely is a key component of this art. Spectators also note how graceful the rolls are and how magnificent they are to watch.

Describing or reading about Aikido is like trying to experience the Grand Canyon by standing at the rim and looking down. Rangers at the Grand Canyon encourage park visitors to take a walk along a trail or hike down a bit to get a sense of the immensity of the canyon. Aikido is like the canyon. To fully appreciate what Aikido offers in the way of providing alternatives to meeting violence with greater violence, try some of the techniques mentioned in this book.

I began studying conflict-crisis intervention in 1983, and this book is among the fruits of my study. Since becoming a Humane Defense instructor that same year, I have expanded my studies into the art of Aikido. In 1990, my Aikido teacher or *Sensei* encouraged me to open a school, or *dojo,* near my home. Wendell Aikido is a traditional dojo that emphasizes ways in which to bring Aikido into our daily lives. Although the techniques presented in this book are not necessarily Aikido techniques, they are philosophically in sync with Aikido, The Way of Peace.

In 1986, I introduced Response, a conflict-crisis intervention model. This training model emphasizes verbal intervention as the primary conflict management tool. Response also uses hands-on techniques derived from Aikido, but unlike Humane

Primary tool – Verbal

Stay Calm Breathe

Defense, it does not use pain compliance to coerce a person to submit.

The Response model has been implemented in public schools, alternative correctional facilities, and human service agencies. Over the past sixteen years, I have worked with people and agencies in every walk of life from the United States Navy to the chamber of commerce. I also began writing articles for *Aikido Today Magazine*. My column, called "Off the Mat," explores the use of Aikido based principles in everyday situations and de-escalation techniques during conflicts.

I will always remain a bit conflicted about my role as one who teaches crisis intervention skills. Although I have accepted my role in this field of study, I truthfully wish that there were a decreasing need for this type of work instead of an increasing need to learn how to manage extremely volatile situations. *world situation*

Many of the scenarios found in this book are based upon my own life experiences as an intervener. I have learned from those experiences that the basic goals of conflict management are universal, regardless of the circumstances. It is my hope that you can use the skills detailed in this work to help keep yourself safe from harm.

About This Book

Choosing to seek nonviolent alternatives to managing conflict takes a lot of courage. It means accepting personal responsibility for your actions, not passing judgment onto others and controlling a "get even" inclination. The techniques described in this work run counter to the "might makes right" mode of conflict management so pervasive in our society today.

This book provides a systematic approach to be used by both professional and nonprofessional crisis interveners for safely managing conflicts. This model is called Goal-Oriented *Model* Intervention. Through a Goal-Oriented Intervention, you will learn to simplify the management of everyday quarrels and flash-point conflicts.

How to Read This Book

Antagonistic, disruptive, volatile, or threatening behaviors and quarrels between groups are examples of conduct that need to be managed and redirected. Conflict management takes place daily in homes, offices, public schools, alternative schools, residential treatment centers, hospitals, and correctional facilities, as well as in other locales.

A societal tendency to compartmentalize work sites and workers promotes a segregated view of conflict management. Regardless of where you work or with whom, you can use techniques introduced in this work. Parental concerns are included.

For the most part, when I have used the word "client," it designates a person (not the intervener) involved in the conflict. If the scenario doesn't appear to coincide with your circumstance, however, you can change it to meet your own needs. For instance, if it says "The client was standing in the hall yelling" and you are not a clinical worker, put in your own designation: "the student," "my son," or "the agitated woman."

The term "intervener" is used throughout the book. By definition, this intervener is any person who chooses to manage a conflict. It does not necessarily imply that the person is working in a professional capacity. Some cases will be noted, however, with a reminder that a technique is meant especially for a professional intervener.

Over the past twenty years, the category of service that falls under the title crisis intervention has been ever growing to include: disaster preparedness, suicide prevention, rape counseling, crisis hot lines, and fire safety, among many others. This book is about quarrels that can escalate into full-blown conflicts and are thus from time to time identified within this work as conflict-crisis.

The Burden of Conflict

What causes conflicts? Miscommunication, fatigue, and stress are everyday factors that can fan the flames of dispute. Key characters involved and the ways they relate to core issues of their particular conflict make every scenario unique. Individually, each of us can make a difference in how conflict will play itself out.

A conflict does not need to be complex itself in order to have a powerful impact on those involved. At minimum, a person may experience hurt feelings and an unwillingness to pursue resolution. Unfortunately, explosive behavior and physical violence have become increasingly commonplace. When a conflict escalates to the point that confusion, lack of direction, or loss of self-control are experienced, there is chaos. *chaos* The resulting crisis can have disastrous effects on all involved.

By and large, most people learn their approach to conflict early in life. Despite its predictability, people get overwhelmed and lose sight of why and how a conflict got started in the first place. Instead of moving through a dispute and seeking resolution, people in conflict tend to get stuck in a crisis mode.

Fight-or-Flight and the Unwarranted Power Granted to Conflict

A person may experience a desire either to join in and fight back verbally or physically or to seek to flee the scene. When one's rational self has been consumed by events at hand, emerging conflict takes on momentum with seemingly supernatural powers.

"I don't know what got into me."

"I just couldn't stop myself."

"Something inside of me snapped!"

"He went ballistic. I didn't recognize him!"

"Everybody joined in and started chanting 'Fight!' 'Fight!'"

It is all too common for people to use conflict as an excuse for their failure to exercise self-control. Conflict is not an entity. If it were, managing its movement and impact would be easier. We could say to conflict, "Ah! There you are. I can see you. Get out of this house right now!"

Dismantling conflict's reign over people's actions begins with revealing the source of its power.

Conflict Makes People Feel Unsafe

To be safe means to be free from the threat of danger, harm, or loss. These three elements are at risk whenever you engage in a conflict.

A conflict that escalates into a physical confrontation, such as a fist fight, is undeniably dangerous. Physical harm is the extreme outcome of this type of conflict. You don't need to feel physically threatened to be in danger, however. Conflict can trigger an emotional response, thereby creating a state of vulnerability. Loss of emotional control and the unpredictability of conflict impact the degree to which people feel safe. Potential conflict is enough to make capable people avoid intercepting even small disputes.

Simplify Conflict

Knowing that conflict makes us feel unsafe helps to clarify the initial goals of conflict management: to secure personal safety and to secure scene safety. Once these two goals are secured, the new goal becomes to help those in conflict regain a sense of self-control, which in turn helps them feel safe.

Avoid the desire to resolve a conflict before all parties involved, including you, feel safe. Finding out, "Who started the argument first?" or discussing the particulars of an incident is a conflict resolution goal, not a conflict management goal. While you are securing scene safety, conflicting parties might resolve their differences. For instance, someone might say, "I didn't mean to call Marcy a jerk. I was upset, and I am sorry for blowing off my steam at her. I hope you accept my apology, Marcy." If Marcy trusts the process, she is likely to accept the apology—something she can do only if she feels safe.

If she didn't accept the apology at that moment, then resolution would have to wait until she and the name caller were willing and able to discuss the dispute without resorting to mean-spirited name calling.

The operative word of conflict management is safety. Learning to ask "Am I safe?" is the first step before fully engaging in a conflict. Making the scene safe is the second goal of conflict management. These two initial steps help to keep you on task. When safety concerns are addressed, conflict becomes approachable and thus manageable.

Self–Leadership Skills

Creating order from chaos without the use of force requires an array of universal conflict management tools. These techniques rely upon your ability to sustain a reasonable amount of self-control and thus self-leadership.

Self-leadership involves making a conscious choice to act in response to conflict. In this context, to act is defined as responding to a conflict without being pulled in emotionally or to remain calm and clearheaded. The use of breathing techniques for maintaining self-control is of the utmost importance. In essence, self-leadership entails choosing to look beyond your self–interest. In the words of Morihei Ueshiba, the founder of Aikido, "True victory is self victory." Changing your approach to conflict is a demanding transformation. The ability to view conflict as neither good nor evil permits you to see through the emotions of the moment and lead conflict out of chaos and toward safety.

Conflict Mgmt. tools
- *self-control*
- *self-leadership*
  - *act in response to conflict*
    - *calm*
    - *clearheaded*
      - *breathing techniq*

"Lead Conflict out of Chaos + toward Safety"

To Prevent

Difficulties are meant to rouse, not discourage. The human spirit is to grow strong by conflict.

—William Ellery Channing

The first type of crisis I learned to respond to was a medical emergency. Early on in undergraduate school, I took a First Responders course and, in my senior year, I became certified as an emergency medical technician (EMT). Over the years, I have noticed how EMT skills overlap with those of a conflict-crisis intervener.

The Feel, Look, Listen Approach

In basic first aid, "Look, Listen, and Feel" is part of every initial assessment. Using the same cues, in the order Feel, Look, and Listen, you can learn to observe indicators of potential conflict. The Feel, Look, and Listen approach to identifying warning indicators is quick and easy to use. From this starting point, indicators that would normally go unnoticed are instead brought to light. Recognizing indicators of an imminent conflict is an essential crisis prevention and conflict management skill.

The following illustration depicts the initial stage of crisis prevention.

Goal-Oriented Intervention Model

CRISIS PREVENTION   ⟶   *Prevent Conflicts from Occurring*
GOAL   *by*
Identifying Potentially Dangerous Indicators
Feel, Look, Listen Approach

---

1) To feel, in this case, implies paying attention to your gut feeling or intuition.

"Mary seemed off to me yesterday. She just wasn't her old self."

"I had a feeling the students were planning something, but I just didn't listen to myself."

Intuition is the subconscious picking up cues. When you have a gut feeling, pay attention to what your body is telling you. If the hairs on the back of your neck start to rise or your stomach is unusually tight and you find yourself in a defensive posture, then your body may be telling you that there is more than meets the eye and it would be best to be on guard.

Parents quickly hone this skill. For instance, a mother or father will be talking to a friend one moment and intuitively turn to catch a child from falling down. "I just sense when something is going to happen to my son."

Conflict is like a tropical storm. You never really know where or when it is going to touch down. Yet, just as we can feel the atmospheric change in the air of an oncoming storm, we are capable of sensing panic or tension in others.

2) To look means visually collecting indicators that are threatening or out of place. How are people posturing themselves? Are they in a defensive position? Do they look scared? When there is a large group of people involved, observe the entire group. Making eye contact with the group at large ensures that you are aware of everyone present, even those who are seemingly uninvolved. In doing so, you offer reassurance that you are aware and in charge. You might notice sub grouping, during which people are moving away from agitators or the group may be unusually quiet and looking away from potential conflict.

Noticing eyes, hands, posture, and feet can help you detect subtleties about what a person is thinking or feeling. Flaring nostrils occur with fear, anger, and frustration. Clenched fists held tightly at the side are indicators of frustration and anxiety. A squared off stance with the feet shoulder width apart may be an indicator of preparedness or intimidation. Shifting feet, pacing, and stomping are often indicators of frustration.

Observing posture helps to identify additional cues. When arms are held straight at the sides, chest out and standing tall, you should be cautious, because that posture may be an indication of readiness for a verbal or physical assault.

3) To listen means staying alert to sounds. Is it unusually loud or quiet? What tone of voice is being used? Is it sharp or threatening, or conciliatory? What is really being said? Are you hearing a lively game of cards being played, or is the joking actually antagonistic or at the expense of someone's well-being?

Integrate the Feel, Look, Listen Approach

Incorporating another tool into your conflict management style usually takes a bit of practice. You may initially view the approach as a one, two, and three process. In reality, though, components should occur concurrently. For example, feel the mood of the room while looking and listening to the way people involved in conflict are interacting.

The Feel, Look, Listen Approach as a crisis prevention technique encourages us to pay attention to warning indicators.

Breathing as An Indicator

In emergencies, first responders feel for a pulse and a patient's breath. In crisis prevention and intervention, the breath is also an important indicator of potential escalation.

flaring nostrals - fear, anger & frustration
Clenched fists - frustration & anxiety

- breathing patterns
frustration
stress
fear

Breath as a subtle yet powerful indicator is too often overlooked during conflict management. With a little practice, you can begin observing breathing patterns for signs of frustration, stress, and fear. For instance, an agitated person will have flared nostrils and will breathe with force. Heavy sighs or the irritated sounding "Psst" as people blow air through their teeth are noticeable indicators of frustration and stress. Withheld and shallow breathing indicates fear. Learning to assess breathing patterns and their associated behaviors is another essential conflict management skill.

When Indicators Are Overlooked

Precautionary measures are taken daily to deter crises in all types of settings. Teachers meet with students and parents to discuss obstacles hindering students' scholastic performance. In residential care settings, direct care staff mediate conflicts between clients before they escalate into full-blown crises. In acute care facilities where patients are already in crisis, staff work one-on-one with patients. Human resource departments in the public and private sector provide employees classes in stress reduction and conflict mediation.

Even with the use of precautionary measures, though, conflicts still occur. The outcome can be catastrophic.

March 6, 2001

Fifteen-year-old Andy Williams shot and killed two people and wounded thirteen at his high school in Santee, California, on March 6, 2001. A month prior to the shooting, Andy had been telling his friends that he was going to take his father's gun and bring it to the school to shoot people. His friends later said that they thought he was joking and didn't take him seriously.

Andy had been at the home of his best friend, Josh Stevens. On March 5, 2001, Chris Reynolds, Josh's mom's boyfriend, asked Andy about the threats. Reynolds stated that he had tried calling Andy's father to tell him about Andy's threat to

squared off stance — preparedness or intimidation

Shifting feet, pacing a stomping — frustration

13

take a weapon to school, but he failed to follow through after getting no answer on the Williams phone.

December 26, 2000

Forty-two-year-old Michael McDermott, a software engineer at Edgewater Technology in Wakefield, Massachusetts, killed seven people on December 26, 2000. After entering his work site, he proceeded to methodically hunt down and shoot seven employees of the e-based firm.

McDermott had been experiencing increasing stress. Early that day, he had learned that his vehicle was being repossessed. Edgewater was also about to garnish his wages to pay back taxes he owed the IRS. Like many potential and actual workplace avengers, he had telltale signs of impending volatility, but no one forecast the tragedy.

March, 1998

A State of Connecticut Lottery employee executed four managers including the executive director in early March 1998 then killed himself after returning from a stress reduction workshop. Coworkers noted in retrospect that he had seemed withdrawn and had never gotten over his disputes with management.

Also in March 1998, thirteen-year-old and eleven-year-old boys shot and killed five people at an Arkansas elementary school. A classmate of the thirteen-year-old recounted a conversation with the boy the day before: "Tomorrow you all find out if you live or die."

"And I said, 'What's that suppose to mean?' And he said I'll find out tomorrow."

Why Are Indicators Overlooked?

Incidents like those described above leave us in despair. The question arises, "What could have been done to prevent such tragedy?" The obvious answer is to pay attention to even the most subtle of indicators.

Odd comments or abrupt changes in behavior should not go unnoticed. Two weeks before the Arkansas ambush, the

Pay attention to SMAll things

thirteen-year-old who had been an avid churchgoer suddenly stopped attending mass.

Being alert and always on the lookout for danger is challenging. Unless it is part of your job, like a lifeguard or patrolman, to be constantly vigilant and on the lookout for warning indicators, some signs will slip through the cracks. Then again, even when potentially dangerous indicators are noticed, many people do not always know what to do and often do nothing. A lack of confidence coupled with inadequate training deters many people from intervening. Whether or not you have enough time to intervene is also a factor.

The following two scenarios illustrate what happens when indicators are noted but interveners don't respond to the signals.

Overwhelmed in the Classroom

As a student teacher, Barbara felt overwhelmed by the responsibilities of managing classroom behaviors of seventh graders. She had enough trouble trying to organize her lesson plan. Therefore, when she overheard a group of boys in her class teasing one of the girls, she figured another, more seasoned, teacher would take notice and know how to stop the behavior. Barbara's classroom supervisor, however, did not take charge of the boy's behavior since she expected Barbara to do so or ask for assistance. The girl being teased finally became exasperated and ended up punching one of the boys in the nose.

Passing the Buck

It was quarter of three when Felicia looked at her watch at the emergency shelter for pregnant teens. Only fifteen minutes more until she would be off duty. She knew there was tension between two of the young women who were sitting in the social room. If she could just keep things quiet till three o'clock, the responsibility would fall to someone else to take care of their conflict.

Felicia was able to scoot out of work at three o'clock sharp. When Judy, the second shift worker, came on to duty, she had to spend two hours de-escalating the conflict between the two women that Felicia had avoided.

Unfortunately, the two preceding scenarios are all too common. Being overwhelmed fosters incompetence. Being unskilled puts those who are in your care at risk. Professional caretakers, like Felicia, who put their own self-interest ahead of others undermine their work site's success. Yet not all people lack the time needed to intervene, nor do they lack the skills in basic conflict management. Why else, then, do capable people still allow conflicts to get the best of them both in their personal lives and at work sites? The reason is that conflict can appear insurmountable, when the ability to make sense of an incident is compromised by our emotions.

Content as an Obstacle

The first step in solving a problem is identifying the cause. As easy as this sounds, it can be an ambitious proposal. The story line of a conflict, what I call the content, is the "Who done it?" or "Who is to blame?" Following the content can cause your emotions to lead you astray.

Breaking through a Mother's Lament

Mary was putting her last load of laundry in the washer when she heard a loud crash. She rushed up from the basement to the first floor and found her three kids: Johnny, four, Jimmy, six, and Joey, eight, staring wide eyed at broken glass on the kitchen floor. Mary saw the boys' football on the floor next to her late grandmother's now broken teapot.

"How many times have I told you boys to keep that football outside?" screamed Mary. "I told your father not to play with you indoors. Oh, God! My mother told me not to leave my good china out where you kids could get to it. Why couldn't I have had three girls instead of boys? Wait till your father gets back from the store."

Luke, Mary's husband, happened to hear Mary's last statement as he walked in through the front door. "What about me?" he called out.

Emotions — get in the way

16

"Luke, I told you not to play with the boys inside. Look what they have done this time. I have been working all morning just so we could go out to the fair this afternoon. This is the thanks I get for working so hard. I can see my hard work is not appreciated." Mary turned and stomped off to her bedroom and said in a low clear voice, "Damn you all."

After Luke directed his sons to clean up the mess, he went to the bedroom door and knocked. "May I come in?" asked Luke.

He heard a small whispered "Yes" and entered.

"Feel like talking?"

"I'm so mad."

"Say more."

"I'm mad at everyone—you, the kids, my mother." Mary let out a small laugh. "God. I can't believe myself sometimes. Where did all that stuff come from? That little teapot was so special to me, Luke. I used to sit with my grandmother drinking tea, and we would both pretend that we were princesses. Isn't that silly?"

"Sounds pretty sweet to me."

"I just lost myself when I saw that it was broken. I feel stupid for not taking my mother's advice."

"No blaming, okay?"

"I feel like I lost of piece of me when I saw the glass on the floor."

Luke actively listened to Mary. The skill of active listening utilizes leading statements that engage the speaker. For example, "Could you say more?" or "Please go on." Active listening may also be nonverbal, as when you nod or shake your head signifying understanding and interest. Because of Luke's active listening and feedback, Mary was able to gain clarity and change her focus from being angry to speaking about the loss of her teapot. If Mary had been unable or unwilling to participate in this conversation, she might have spent the rest of the day in her bedroom sulking.

Learning to drop the content, the "Who done it?" or the "Who is to blame?", can help identify the root of one's emotional outburst. In Mary's case she realized that seeing her broken teapot caused her anguish. By actively listening, Luke helped her to drop the content. Dropping the content as a preventive measure helps to reveal harmful behaviors. Being explosive and lashing out, as Mary did, serves no one. After dropping the content, she was able to reflect upon her behavior and find a less destructive response while still acknowledging her feelings.

Regretting the incident after she was able to drop the content, Mary might say, "I can't believe what I said to the kids, Luke. I told them that I wished I had girls, instead of boys. What was I thinking? My anger got the best of me. If I had told them how sad I was to see the teapot was broken, I know they would be more careful next time. Instead they only saw me at my worst. I don't like them saying mean things to each other. I have to try not to do the same thing myself."

Dropping the content can be done by yourself or with the help of another person. For instance, sometimes I say "Drop the content" to myself. By mentally stepping back from the scene that is unfolding, I am often able to remain non-reactive and cut to the source of potential conflict. Instead of a sterile response to the situation or a reactive response, I find that my objective self is able to make a better connection with those involved than when I allow my emotions to guide me. Clarity is a powerful perspective that draws in those who lack stability.

In Aikido I train to project a non-reactive posture. I stand with my hands down along my side and my feet slightly offset so that one foot is forward. My knees stay flexed, and I usually have a smile on my face, not a grimace. This stance looks completely nonthreatening. In effect, I drop the content of potential conflict by standing in an open posture, eliciting dialogue. It can disarm an attacker when the object of the attack stands in an open posture that exudes confidence and clarity.

Thus, Aikido teaches a way to drop the physical content of a conflict that may be displayed through body language.

Loose the Emotions

Active listening is a similar technique that can create a way to drop the content in a conflict. The following is a glimpse of two different conversations where content is an obstacle and active listening helps to drop the content.

Unveiling a Holiday Drama

"When my sister walked into the room, I felt my forehead begin to sweat," Christopher told Lisa, his housemate. "I couldn't believe she was there! And she brought her new boyfriend! She is always waltzing in with someone new, like she owns the whole world. All she ever gives my family is this one little three-hour blast at Christmas. My parents rag on me every time she leaves. I'm always left picking up all the pieces for her, trying to settle down my mother and father, who keep asking me where they went wrong."

Once Christopher quieted down, Lisa asked him if he wanted to say more about his sister.

"I don't know. I just feel so upset by it all."

"What's the real issue here, Chris?" Lisa asked.

"This stuff between us is so old. Things are never gonna change between her and me."

In the exchange, Lisa encouraged Chris to drop the content. Chris asked, "What do you mean?"

"Being with family can kick up a lot of old feelings. You get a kind of snowball effect. Everything is all mushed together. Squeeze out the essentials." Lisa explained.

"Meaning what?" said Chris.

"Meaning?" Lisa went on. "Start at the beginning. You said your forehead began to sweat when your sister walked into the room. Was that because she had a new boyfriend or because you were worrying about your folks, or what?"

Chris made a small, sad laugh and said, "I just miss her. I miss my sister! She was the one I depended on."

Dropping the content takes courage because conflict impacts us on an emotional level. It would have been easier for Chris to continue to gripe about his sister than to be vulnerable by admitting that he missed her. Venting requires no individual responsibility for your part in a conflict, and you can complain about another person or group until the sun sets tomorrow. Dropping the content, however, does require self-assessment and the ability to accept responsibility for your own role in a conflict.

Instead of judging his sister's actions by saying or thinking, "She is always waltzing in with someone new, like she owns the whole world," dropping the content for Chris required him to assess his own actions about his sister: "I just miss her. I miss my sister!" Perhaps next time he saw his sister he could avoid getting mad and instead try a different tack that might include a request to renew their friendship or simply tell her, "I miss you."

A Couple's Quarrel

As soon as Nicole got into her best friend Maria's car, she began to recount her recent saga with Tony. "I know I told him that my mother was visiting, you see, but he doesn't listen to me. So the next thing I know, he is stomping around upstairs making my life miserable. He is all upset because she is still there and supposedly we are expected for dinner at our friend's, Pete and Sue's. How would I know that he made plans for us to go out? He acts like a baby. I can't stand it. We hardly spoke to each other for the rest of the evening!"

"Wow," Maria said. "You guys aren't getting along."

Nicole replied, "What do you think I'm trying to tell you? Isn't it obvious? He just doesn't include me in on anything. I'm supposed to be his wife, but I feel more like a slave."

Although venting about a conflict can be healthy, it has a tendency to be destructive, like Mary's outburst over the teapot. Redirecting Nicole away from this path could help her to prevent conflict with Tony from escalating or recurring.

"Is this about your mom?" inquired Maria.

"I wish it was that easy," said Nicole.

"Is it about Pete and Sue?"

"No. I love those guys. And we did go over once my mom left."

"So, what do you think this argument was about?" encouraged Maria.

Keep the Communication always open.

"All our arguments are about the same thing. He doesn't talk to me. And I don't talk to him. I guess we never really took time to talk, even when we first got together," said Nicole in a sad and quiet tone.

In this last statement, Nicole identified a key point of her distress: "He doesn't talk to me. And I don't talk to him. " Their inability to communicate will likely continue to impact their lives. Revealing a harmful pattern is a first step in finding a solution and preventing the behavior from recurring. Nicole could seek individual counseling for improving her own communication skills, but it is likely that she would want her husband to make a commitment to work on his skills too. If Nicole said to Tony, "We have lousy communication skills," it is likely that Tony would become defensive and disagree: "I don't know what you are talking about. I communicate just fine." Like Chris, Nicole should have stated her role and let Tony take responsibility for himself: "Tony, I would like to work on the way I communicate with you. I am not sure how to do this. I am going to need your help. Would you be willing to set aside some time this week after dinner to help me out?" Tony could then decide his part in Nicole's attempt to better their relationship.

The next vignettes illustrate how workers at care facilities could benefit from dropping the content. Although these may appear very site-specific, the same scenario with a different cast of characters can be found in many homes and other work sites.

Steve's Socks

Every Wednesday like clockwork at the adult mental health residential treatment center, Steve had an explosive outburst when he finished his laundry. He said, "Who took my T-shirt?" or "Hey! One of my socks is missing!" Steve had been known to go barging into other residents' rooms, slinging profanities and demanding to check their drawers.

Staff and residents alike were fed up with his behavior. "We have tried everything: marking his clothes, giving him a special basket for his laundry, and even staying with him while he washes his clothes. Nothing seems to work."

The effort had focused solely on keeping Steve's clothes intact. Without dropping the content, everyone was overlooking a harmful behavior, which was how Steve handled his anger. Steve might never be happy with his clothes, so that wasn't the real point. One day he might find that he has all his articles but a sweater shrank or colors ran, and his temper would erupt again.

Exposing a harmful behavior, like Steve's unbridled anger, is a starting point. In all likelihood, the same behavior would arise again. Additional guidance would be required to help remind him how to manage his anger.

Sheryl's Work Site Behavior

Sheryl was a fast, articulate talker. She was also known as an antagonist and was typically found in the middle of conflicts, either egging on two other parties or intimidating someone else.

Mrs. Lewis had just been told that Sheryl was transferred to her department at Community Insurance Incorporated. She was also told that Sheryl rambled on and on when she was angry and had difficulty listening to anyone until she had settled down. Once she had controlled her anger, however, she was a good listener and one of CII's best workers. Mrs. Lewis was scheduled to meet her to discuss her new job duties.

When someone hears statements like "Sheryl is a manipulator and could talk her way out of a bag," it is hard not to pass judgment before meeting. The tendency is to discuss the behavior and not the precipitant of the behavior. If Mrs. Lewis were to begin their meeting discussing Sheryl's behavior, Sheryl would surely take the defensive.

Sheryl, like Steve, needed to learn how to manage anger. Mrs. Lewis could use the qualities needed for her new job placement as the vehicle for discussing Sheryl's communication and anger management skills. Learning to manage harmful behavior helps those in perpetual conflict understand potential obstacles to their success.

Starting a Dialogue with Sheryl

Once they had gone through the basic introductory hellos, Mrs. Lewis began by saying, "Sheryl, we are meeting this morning to speak about your new duties here at CII. You are a skilled worker, and this position will be an exciting new challenge. What were you hoping to bring to this new team?"

"I am a good listener and love to work hard on new ideas," said Sheryl.

"Could you say more about your attributes as a good listener?" inquired Mrs. Lewis. "I am expecting you to be a leader, and I know that role can have its ups and downs."

Mrs. Lewis left the door open for Sheryl to begin discussing her strengths. She also directed the conversation toward communication skills and the dynamics of a team, instead of confronting Sheryl by saying, "I know you have a hard time working with others." Mrs. Lewis put Sheryl in the driver's seat. "Could you say more?" was an enticing request that allowed Sheryl to reflect upon her work style and communication skills.

Recurring Conflict Due to Repetitive Behavior

Many everyday behaviors, like squabbling with others or failing to communicate needs in a non-confrontational manner, can't be changed overnight, and certainly won't be changed by merely demanding that a person "shape up or ship *Class* out." Bear in mind that most people are doing the best they can with the tools they have. Until you are guided toward another way to respond to a difficult situation, you will keep going back to what is most familiar.

Teach Them How

Repetitive behavior is an underlying cause of many conflicts. Such behavior is easily masked by circumstances surrounding conflict. Until one's behavior is changed or redirected, conflict will continue, often with increasing intensity.

The following list highlights common conflicts caused by repetitive behavior. Again, these behaviors can be translated into many different settings.

Examples of repetitive behavior:
- a family member who always disrupts a dinner
- a client who continually disrupts group meetings
- a son who abuses car privileges by leaving the tank empty after each use
- a resident at a treatment facility who abuses telephone privileges every time by staying on the line longer than the time allocated
- a student who disrupts the class every day by distracting other students
- a patient who constantly demands to have her medication or cigarettes
- a student who regularly fights during recess
- an employee who is always late or calling in sick for work

Creating an Action Plan

Creating an action plan for repetitive behavior prevents conflicts from recurring. Creating an action plan is a proactive measure to take for those who seek to move beyond the crippling and at times explosive effect of repetitive behavior. For instance, if you find yourself always losing your temper, an action plan can help you manage your anger before it gets explosive.

The time to create an action plan is not when you are in the middle of an argument or going to the activity that repeatedly triggers unwanted behaviors. Think of yourself when you are angry and in conflict. Can you really listen to someone who might have good advice? Probably not, because you are already thinking of the difficult conversation that you are about to have. The time to work on an action plan is when the person in need is able to listen and commit to a new course of action. If there are conflicting parties needing to work through a conflict, they have to be composed and willing to engage with each other. Learning to take responsibility for our actions is an important life skill.

New Course of Action !!!
Need One

Timing for a Professional Intervener

It takes enormous self-control to stop right before going through the door to a difficult conversation. If it is hard for staff to do, it is even harder for clients, whose self-control is already challenged. They will only learn to shift their response to a situation by being offered skilled guidance. Creating an action plan is like being a professional wilderness guide. You must prepare, set up, and instruct using the proper tools and techniques to ensure a rewarding first adventure and avoid an experience in misery.

find Some

The following protocols are key components when creating an action plan.

Active Listening

- Demonstrate that you are sincerely interested in what is being said.
- Practice dropping the content.
- The solution becomes clear once a harmful behavior is revealed.
- Pay attention to your intuition.

If you get a hunch that the conflict is being fueled by repetitive behavior, take note.

Timing Your Intervention

Managing repetitive behavior requires timing your intervention so that the person you are trying to help is willing and able to listen.

Let's revisit some of our friends from a few pages back and see how the timing of the intervention impacted them.

- Mary needed a little time alone before she could speak to Luke.
- Christopher needed to emote before he could make sense of his conflict with his sister.
- Nicole needed to talk with someone other than Tony in order to gain clarity on her marriage.
- Mrs. Lewis timed her intervention by moving into the discussion slowly with Sheryl instead of bringing up her behavior as the first subject.

A person in conflict who is hampered by repetitive behavior has to be able and willing to listen to alternatives. It is in no one's best interest to begin such a dialogue when emotions are still highly charged.

What follows is an example of purposeful timing of an intervention in order to make a collaborative action plan for managing a student's behavior.

Recess with Hector

Hector, a fifth grader at Pine Street Elementary School, frequently got into fights with other students at recess. He was given a number of detentions, and teachers had been meeting with his mother without Hector present to discuss his behavior.

During the Monday afternoon teacher's meeting, Ms. Smith, his new homeroom teacher, asked if anyone had discussed with Hector what he could or couldn't hear from a teacher when he was getting upset. "We all have buttons that are easily pushed when someone says just the right word to get us going. I wonder if we are saying the wrong thing to him," Ms. Smith said to the others, and then she volunteered to ask him.

Wednesday afternoon during the detention period, Ms. Smith asked Hector to come up to her desk. "Hector, I need your help tomorrow," she said.

"What do you mean?" asked Hector.

"Well," replied Ms. Smith, "I keep blowing it, saying all the wrong things to you when you are at recess."

"My mom said our whole family has a temper. Don't worry about it," said Hector with a sheepish grin.

"When you are getting upset, is there anything that your mom says or someone else says that helps you think about what you are doing? Come on Hector, tell me something that will make you smile like you are doing now. I know you want to do the right thing," urged Ms. Smith.

"If you want to say something to me, how about, 'Do the right thing'? I like that," said Hector.

"Okay. Next time during recess if I see that you are getting upset with a classmate, I'm going to say 'Hector, do the right thing.' When I say that, I would like you to look right at me and nod your head and then take two steps back away from whomever you are talking to. Sounds kind of silly, huh? But I think it might work. Are you willing to try it?" asked Ms. Smith.

Hector agreed to try. The playground disputes decreased after that initial meeting with Hector. Ms. Smith was pleased to hear Hector say, "Do the right thing" whenever he ran by her on his way out to recess.

Identifying recurring behavior and meeting with a person when he or she is willing or able to listen is all part of how you create an action plan. People, regardless of their history, have times when they are receptive to hearing and discussing things in a rational way. Finding that moment takes time and patience but is well worth the effort.

Let's revisit Steve and see how an action plan could be created to help him manage his anger.

Steve's Action Plan

On Monday, two days before Steve did his laundry, Kevin, a worker at Steve's site, set up a meeting time with Steve for two in the afternoon, a quiet time when the television wasn't on. Steve usually spent his time reading in his room. He was excited about the meeting with Kevin, which he understood was an opportunity to discuss his laundry.

At exactly two o'clock, Steve was outside Kevin's office knocking to come in. Kevin rose up out of his chair, opened the door for Steve, and greeted him by saying, "Hi, Steve. Please take a seat here next to my desk." Kevin usually just called out, "Come in." Instead, Kevin tried to set a pace that was formal, hoping that Steve would follow his lead and act less frantic and more businesslike.

Steve smiled and took a seat. Kevin said, "I want to begin by thanking you for taking the time to meet with me this afternoon. I know this is your free time. I have some ideas about laundry day that I think might help you."

"Good, good," Steve said. "You have my full attention. I have some thoughts too, like letting me do my laundry first. I'll get up early and get it done before breakfast."

"Wow," Kevin replied. "That is a pretty gracious offer. I am willing to explore that idea."

The two men discussed the morning routine, and Kevin noticed how thoroughly Steve made plans to get up before the rest of the group. He said he would let Steve try doing his laundry early Wednesday morning. They agreed to meet later in the day and review how things went.

Kevin then asked Steve to set up an action plan if there were a problem with his laundry that morning. "This action plan is much like what you presented to me, but it is designed to deal with any problems that may occur. I want you to be successful and get your laundry done without any hitches. For instance, what if the machine doesn't work right or the last person using it left it dirty? How would you manage that?"

Kevin noticed Steve's face had tensed up and his face was flushed. "I'm with you, Steve. Keep breathing," Kevin said.

Steve let out a small breath of air and looked down at the floor.

"What you are doing right now may help this Wednesday," Kevin added.

Bewildered, Steve looked up at Kevin.

"Notice how you are breathing and thinking about what I said? That is great. You're taking your time and controlling your emotions. I know you can do that if a problem arises with your laundry."

"I guess," said Steve.

Kevin continued to engage Steve in designing a plan for managing his reaction to problems that might arise when he did his laundry.

Over the next few months, Kevin maintained an atmosphere of appreciation toward Steve for continuing to manage his behavior while directing him to look at obstacles that impeded his success. Taking time to pave a path toward success is a crucial step in the creation of a workable action plan for managing harmful behaviors. First, of course, both parties need to agree about what a successful outcome is. The common goal for Kevin and Steve was to get the laundry done and to manage laundry mishaps, like a lost sock, without Steve becoming explosive.

The next vignette will present you with three options for managing a harmful behavior. Each option is viable, but only one will truly help Jerome manage his repetitive behavior.

Jerome's Phone Call

Every Monday night at the emergency shelter for adolescents, Jerome called his father. Sharon, the second shift supervisor, could set her clock by the moment that Jerome finally got upset at his father's tirade and slammed the receiver down, turning his anger on the other residents in the hallway. Sharon said, "Jerome gets in everybody's face, and once I almost had to call the police to come and assist me when Jerome was refusing to come in off the front lawn one night after a call. He was kicking over the garbage cans in our driveway and cussing. I can't let that type of behavior occur in a residential neighborhood. I also can't prevent him from talking to his Dad. I just don't know what to do."

Which action plan is a good approach for Jerome?

Option 1

Sharon knew that Jerome got mad whenever he talked to his Dad on the phone. So, while Jerome waited in the social room to make his call in fifteen minutes, Sharon asked him into the office to discuss other ways to work with the difficult telephone call.

Option 2

Sharon told Jerome that he had to call his father on Friday afternoon when fewer residents were in the shelter instead of Monday nights when the shelter was full. Sharon and the rest of the treatment team decided that the next time Jerome had an angry outburst due to his phone calls with his Dad, he would be fully reprimanded and come down one point, which could take away his eligibility to go to the movie theater that weekend.

Sharon decided to talk to Jerome on Friday about his Monday night phone call. Jerome always got back from work on Fridays fifteen minutes before everyone else, so they would have privacy, and Jerome's confidentiality would be protected. During the meeting, Sharon asked Jerome what happened every time he talked with his Dad on Monday nights. "Oh, I don't know, Sharon," Jerome replied. "He always calls me a loser or something."

"What do you do when he calls you a loser?" inquired Sharon.

"You mean the way I get mad?" asked Jerome. Sharon nodded and Jerome went on, "Well, I can't stand it when he gets on my case, so I just hang up."

Sharon and Jerome then discussed what to do when he got fed up listening to his dad. They worked through a role-play of Jerome talking on the phone with his dad and agreed to meet at least fifteen minutes before the phone call on Monday to reaffirm their new strategy.

The goal of creating an action plan is to find a way that will help the other person be successful. The real issue is teaching Jerome to manage his anger, not whether he calls his father on Friday or Monday. Sharon might be able to give some guidance over the long term in relation to his father, but in the short term, her goal is to help Jerome learn how to manage his anger. Therefore, Option 3 is the strategy with the most potential to help Jerome.

The next illustration outlines the completion of the crisis prevention goal after dropping the content by creating an action plan.

Summary: Living Is Hard Work

Meeting day-to-day needs of food and shelter is only the tip of the iceberg in terms of what each of us needs to survive if we are to actively engage in life. If you're not living off the

goal - action plan - help other be successful

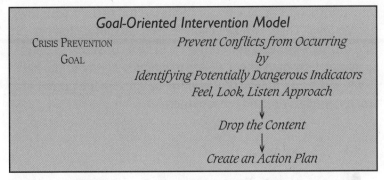

Goal-Oriented Intervention Model

CRISIS PREVENTION   *Prevent Conflicts from Occurring*
GOAL   *by*
Identifying Potentially Dangerous Indicators
Feel, Look, Listen Approach
↓
Drop the Content
↓
Create an Action Plan

land in total isolation, you are going to need communication skills, and getting along with others is not always going to be trouble-free. Conflict happens. The important thing to remember is that you are able to have an impact on how conflict affects your life.

(1)   The Feel, Look, Listen Approach is an accessible technique for observing potentially dangerous indicators. It provides a vantage point for observing escalating behavior. Being prepared for conflict feels a whole lot better than being paranoid and consumed by the fear of impending conflict.

(2)   Removing the melodrama associated with so many conflicts is also a skill that requires observation and active listening. Dropping the content removes drama and helps reveal harmful behaviors that can become repetitive and contribute to recurring or escalating conflicts.

(3)   One of the best investments in conflict prevention is having an action plan that helps manage potential crisis or harmful behaviors. You should create workable action plans. Begin with small increments of success, ensuring a strong foundation. Avoid making action plans that are too complex. *Simple*

There will be conflicts and crises that come on unexpectedly. Your preparedness for handling everyday squabbles and mini crises will come in handy during such times. In Aikido, we practice the same technique over and over. I relish the feeling of taking control of my life and being actively engaged in everything that I do.

My mom taught me a saying when I was a fourteen and struggling like many teenagers when they are slowly moving into adulthood. "Don't let your highs get too high or your lows get too low." There will be obstacles that each of us have to face during our lives, and conflict will be a constant. In order to manage my own anger, I keep my mom's saying in the back of my mind and realize that seeking balance in life takes hard work, compassion, and preparedness.

Balance = hard work - compassion a preparedness

Am I Safe?

If you cry "Forward," you must make plain in what direction to go.

—Anton Chekov

As a consultant and trainer in conflict management, I have an opportunity to work with a diverse cross section of professional and nonprofessional interveners. This position has afforded me a bird's eye view of how people manage conflict. One of the most consistent observations I have made is that many people get stuck during conflict management role-plays. "I don't know what to do" is a common statement from those too overwhelmed by a conflict they were supposed to be managing.

Knowing what to say and what not to say are some of the leading concerns people have in the midst of a volatile situation. "Why me?" or "How did this start?" or "Why didn't I see it coming?" are distracting internal dialogues for people overcome by a conflict. Pertinent as such questions may be, they can rarely be answered during a conflict. The important question is, "What am I supposed to do?"

Debunking the "Que Sera, Sera" Conflict Management Style

When a role-player is stuck and unable to manage a conflict, I ask, "What is your goal?" The range of responses varies from, "What do you mean?" to "My goal is to stop the conflict." When I ask how people expect to stop the conflict besides using brute force, there is often no set plan. In other words they are "winging it."

Making it through "by the seat of your pants" is neither safe nor effective. Would you want a fire department or paramedic responding haphazardly to your needs? Imagine yourself needing emergency medical care and first responders beginning cardiopulmonary resuscitation (CPR) when what you really need is a splint on your leg!

Granted, not everyone is a professional crisis intervention specialist. Still, integrating a goal-setting approach into your intervention style shows good common sense and is a universal conflict management skill.

The primary goal for all conflict or crisis interventions is to attain safety. Safety is broken down into two stages: personal safety and scene safety. When you feel personally safe from harm, you will think more clearly and remain emotionally unaffected by angry words directed at you. You are also likely to exhaust your breadth of verbal responses before resorting to a physical response. With scene safety, you take into account physical factors such as furniture, exit routes, and tight quarters that can hinder management of a conflict.

Safety First, Resolution Later

Although wanting to stop a conflict may be a first inclination, it bypasses the necessity of safeguarding yourself and others. Perhaps with brute force you *could* physically stop another person from pummeling someone else. An authority figure like a parent or police officer could demand someone to stop their actions. But for many, brute force is not an option, and, although you may stop a person for a moment, you are not addressing the actual conflict. The thing to remember is that crisis intervention and crisis resolution are two separate and distinct steps that typically happen in sequence—they are rarely simultaneous. If you strive for immediate resolution to a conflict, you may find yourself inadvertently exacerbating the overall crisis.

Crisis resolution as a primary goal is impractical, since resolution cannot be achieved until all parties feel safe. Expecting a person to think coherently when in distress only generates more frustration. Most people need time to clear their thoughts before they can make sense of a conflict. Deciphering who is responsible for whatever just happened should take place later, when people involved are able to listen to each other.

All of the interveners in the previous chapter were able to begin to help others seek a solution to their conflicts only when the person in conflict was composed and willing to listen to another person's point of view. Making sure Steve was a willing participant in the discussion, Kevin was very methodical in the way he talked to Steve about his behavior when doing his laundry. Maria let Nicole "vent" about her dispute with Tony first before she was able to make some sense out of her marital problems. Luke gave Mary some private time alone before he went to speak with her about the broken teapot. If he had demanded that she stay in the room with her boys and discuss the matter, she might have continued to spout mean spirited statements like she had earlier: "I wish I had had three girls instead of boys." Like Maria with Nicole, Lisa listened to her friend Christopher emote about his family dynamics before asking him the leading questions that directed him toward dropping the content. Ms. Smith met with Hector during a quiet time, when he was able to listen to her idea about managing his behavior during recess.

Resolution can occur only when those in conflict have had time to regain a sense of self-control. The focus during management of an intervention is to create safety for all parties. Giving people a little space to vent or be alone or away from the scene of the incident may provide instant relief and a renewed sense of well-being.

focus - Safety for all

The following vignette is an illustration of what can happen when interveners try to stop a conflict before securing personal safety and scene safety.

Ricky and John's Fight

Ricky and John Martin were pushing each other in the Martins' backyard. The pushing quickly turned into punching. Their parents both ran to the scene from opposite directions, with Mr. Martin arriving first. While separating the two boys, Mr. Martin asked, "Okay, who started it?"

Both boys screamed out in unison, "He did!" and then, "You liar!"

Like Mr. Martin, your first inclination during conflict management may be to find out what happened. In other words, you try resolving the crisis before the scene is totally safe for everyone. In fact, Mr. Martin's questioning of his two sons should have taken place only after Ricky and John had been separated and given time to settle down.

Interventions like this one take place every day, with a person trying to resolve the conflict first. But such interventions involve a level of coercion providing only a short-term solution. Instead, you should emphasize safety and provide an alternative to the "might-makes-right" style of confrontational conflict management.

Addressing Ricky and John's Personal Safety

People are less inclined to be truthful or willing to compromise when they feel threatened. Giving each boy some time alone away from his brother might facilitate Ricky and John's individual needs to be personally safe from harm. The conflict management goal of securing personal safety and scene safety is an important prerequisite for sound crisis resolution.

Instead of asking the two boys, "Who started the fight?" Mr. Martin could instead begin by saying, "Okay, let's all settle down."

Then he could either direct the boys to take a "time-out" or, if they were visibly de-escalating, he might be able to walk them away from the immediate scene. Finding a neutral location like a picnic table or other sitting area could help to set the mood for discussing the fight and also allow the warring parties to work things out under implied supervision. Then Mr. Martin could ask the boys to speak one at a time and set a goal for them. "We are a family," he could say, "and sometimes we don't get along. Still, it is hard to see my two sons fighting. Let's try talking about what happened without being mean to each other." He could ask each boy if he agrees to work with his brother: "Ricky, are you willing to discuss this matter now?" and then, "John, how about you? Can you discuss this matter now, also?" Such an approach would set an expected norm of civility for the ensuing discussion.

Mr. Martin could also state what the goal of the discussion was: To work through a conflict without being mean. Helping his family learn problem-solving early on is a life skill that will take them through adulthood.

Like the previous situation, not all interventions are high risk for the intervening party. Yet, many people work at sites where personal safety can be threatened. The following vignette illustrates what can happen when the intervener's personal safety is at risk and the intervener is focused more on stopping the conflict than on ensuring personal and scene safety.

Forsaking Personal Safety During an Intervention

It was the second class period of the day at City High. Mr. Smith was taking his turn to check the bathrooms for kids trying to sneak a smoke. As he approached the door, he could hear muffled voices in what sounded like an argument. His palms felt sweaty, and his pulse quickened as he flung the doors open and walked into the bathroom. "All I can remember is the lights going out and something hitting me hard on my head," Mr. Smith said after he was rescued. "After that, I just blacked out."

A drug transaction had been going on in the bathroom when Mr. Smith entered. He hadn't thought twice about his own safety. If he had checked for personal safety and scene safety, however, the scenario would have looked like this. It was the second class period of the day at City High, and Mr. Smith was taking his turn to check the bathroom for kids trying to sneak a smoke. As he approached the door, he heard muffled voices that sounded like an argument. He took a moment to listen outside the door and slow himself down, since he noticed his palms were sweaty and his heart was pounding. Determining that it was indeed an argument, Mr. Smith waved to Mr. Dempsey, a teacher who was monitoring the hall. He put his hands together to form a T and mouthed the word "trouble."

Listen it!

Mr. Dempsey nodded his head that he understood, grabbed the phone inside his room, and called the main office. Mr. Dempsey then came closer to the bathroom. Mr. Smith opened the door with his foot and yelled into the bathroom, "Come on out in the hall, boys! Now!"

Pausing outside the bathroom door and evaluating the level of risk kept Mr. Smith from rushing in and trying to intervene in a scene that was unsafe. Confined and crowded space, such as a bathroom with multiple hiding places for would-be attackers, requires a team approach. Even with additional staff, the police might need to be called. Most crisis intervention trainings for teachers do not teach advanced physical management skills, such as escorting a person out of a confined space that could turn into a riot scene. Remember, it takes only a small crowd to create disorder.

Managing multiple would-be attackers requires advanced skills in physical management. Most teachers are authorized to use only two-person escorts, which means each teacher is holding one of the student's arms. When a room is filled with highly agitated people and you have only two interveners responding, it is not realistic to think that you can hold one person safely and expect the rest of the group to stand by, unless you are a police officer. A uniformed police officer projects authority. Police officers certainly must still be wary, but they are granted more authority than the average citizen or teacher. That authority is embodied in the uniform.

Be cautious of the "I-can-take-care-of-myself" attitude. There is always risk of injury involved when a conflict requires hands-on interventions. Calculate the potential dangers of a situation before entering a scene by yourself. Investigating criminal activity is best left to qualified professionals in law enforcement. If you are expected to catch a person in the act of committing a crime, however, you should have the proper training for such high risk situations. Waiting for the students to come out of the bathroom on their own accord reduces the overall risk of harm for both the teachers and the students.

Self-control

Assessing your own level of self-control is the first step when you are working toward personal safety and overall scene safety. Dick Guere, a friend and teacher who worked in a prison, taught me the following: "If you are not in control of yourself, you are destined to be controlled by others." *Get Help!!*

It is easy to say, "Get a grip on yourself!" or, "You have got to get control of yourself," but what does that really mean? Self-control is the ability to exercise restraint over your own impulses, emotions, or desires.

Am I Safe?

Although your first reaction may be to run directly into a room where two people are arguing, it may not be the safest choice nor the most effective. Once a conflict has begun, you must make sure that you can intervene safely. The following illustration shows what to do after asking, "Am I safe?"

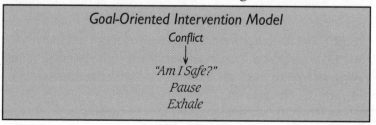

Goal-Oriented Intervention Model
Conflict
↓
"Am I Safe?"
Pause
Exhale

Pause

The pause and exhale are two techniques that should always be done during the initial stage of intervention. A pause can take up to five seconds and is done simply by stopping yourself before entering the scene of a conflict. For example, after entering a room where you hear loud and angry voices, you would stand just inside the doorway for a moment without speaking. This is a time for gauging your own level of self-control. The pause can have a calming effect on those observing by projecting that you are in charge.

The subtle yet powerful technique of pausing before engaging in a conflict shows that the intervener is comfortable with silence. A silent moment can feel awkward if constant interaction is the norm, but it is nevertheless effective. Before practicing for the first time with an angry person, try it during a casual conversation. Simply stand quietly inside the doorway upon entering a room, and notice how heads will turn.

The pause offers a moment to gain control of your breathing and to notice how you are carrying your body. You might find your shoulders are pulled up to your ears, indicating tension. I have noted over the years that many women hold their arms folded and close to their chest. Men, on the other hand, will hold their arms down in front of their groin. Either position can be perceived as a protective stance.

Protecting yourself can be done by maintaining a neutral stance, such as the mediator stance, that facilitates discussion and does not emit readiness for potential combat.

Mediator's Stance

The mediator's stance is a standing position that provides a nonthreatening appearance as well as protection from possible attacks. The mediator's stance typically elects a left foot forward position because most people are right-handed. When people strike out, they are likely to lead with the dominant side, which is usually the right. When intervening with a known left-handed person a right foot forward stance is advised. If you sense potential physical danger, preventive measures like a left foot forward stance protects the most vulnerable part of your body—the vital organs and the face.

Knees should be partially flexed. A slight bend in the knees makes it easier to move in toward a person or away. Imagine a ball player up at bat. Because the player is expected to run right after hitting the ball, there is a deep flex in the knees. The ball player's deep bend is not necessary for everyday conflict, though. A slight flex will do.

You should keep your hands level with your waistline. As for what to do with your hands, I prefer loosely grasping my hands without interlocking my fingers. I also find that holding my palms up as if holding a large book is an open and nonthreatening gesture.

Positioning yourself at forty-five degrees to the person with whom you are speaking provides a space for the agitated person to exit. When you physically block the way for a person to leave the room, as you would in a face-to-face confrontation, you compromise safety.

Self-control is never more critical than during a crisis. Even if they don't seem to show it, people who are involved in the crisis as well as the onlookers are counting on you as intervener to act with self-assurance. This expectation applies to everyone, from parents to cashiers to fire-fighters and human service workers. Your stance as well as your ability to speak with a clear and steady voice directly impact how those in conflict perceive your ability to manage a crisis.

Self-control at the Car Accident

As an EMT since 1981, I have been the first responder at the scenes of many car accidents. During times of intense crises, I have learned the value of maintaining self-control.

I was on the way to visit my parents when traffic began to slow and I realized that there was an accident up ahead. I was able to safely weave my way closer and park my car. Grabbing my case with medical supplies, I ran toward the scene and noticed that no official emergency vehicles were there yet. As I approached, I saw two damaged cars, one burning with people scattering away from it. I also noticed uninjured people who I assumed had come from the nearby homes to help accident victims. I stood for a moment and took in the scene. Taking a couple of slow deep breaths, I tried to plan my next move.

It would be about ten minutes before the first of four ambulances arrived. There were seven people injured. The most seriously injured were four Chinese exchange students who spoke little English. Their car had been hit by a drunk driver who had a baby and another passenger in her car.

I began going from injured person to injured person and assessing their medical needs. When the ambulances finally arrived, I relayed the information to each of the four teams. The scene was chaotic, with the injured moaning from pain, so I reminded the caregivers to take slow deep breaths so they would not get agitated themselves.

Once the injured were on their way to the hospital, I sat down off to the side. Slowly, all the nonprofessionals who were helping at the scene when I first arrived approached me. They thanked me for my help and guidance. I had thought that I was an invisible caretaker unnoticed in the flurry of other emergency workers. I was surprised to hear how I had helped the Samaritans focus on the task instead of getting caught up in the intensity of the disaster scene. They had noticed me when I first entered and stood to evaluate the scene. That presence of mind had set me apart. My calm had enabled others to find a quiet place where they could function effectively. It served as a reminder that the crisis could and would be managed.

Any frantic energy I had felt slowed with my pause at the point of entry into the accident scene. The impact of my pause was greater than I had expected and touched other care givers who also needed reassurance.

Exhale
A slow and deliberate exhale is done simultaneously with the pause. Exhaling is a kick-start for the respiratory system to supply oxygen to the brain. When we are agitated or fearful, we tend to hold our breath or take only short, shallow breaths. When we are intervening, both the quality and

quantity of breath taken can impact critical decision-making. The brain needs oxygen for clear thinking. Deep and deliberate breathing helps us to remain calm and clearheaded.

When I first started teaching courses in crisis intervention, I would say "Remember to breathe." I found over time, though, that most people inhale first when they think, "Breathe." Inhaling during a critical event like a conflict does not necessarily mean you will automatically exhale. As long as your body has air, your reflex to exhale may be delayed for a moment. You could continue to hold your breath for quite a long time, even while speaking. Holding your breath is not quality breathing. Your lungs would prefer to have a fresh and consistent supply of oxygen. Ideally, you want to continue to breathe slowly, in and out, while making your intervention.

Now, instead of saying "Remember to breathe," I remind interveners. "Remember to exhale." You will probably need to inhale first, but by focusing on the exhale, your respiratory system will automatically inhale. Once I exhale, I find it very difficult to speak without taking time to inhale.

In any intervention, personal safety is your first priority. With safety as your measuring stick, you know clearly when to enter or exit an intervention. You risk your own safety and that of others when you go blindly into a conflict without thinking first, "Am I safe?" The following chart shows what to do next.

Goal-Oriented Intervention Model
Conflict
↓
"Am I Safe?"
Pause
Exhale
↓
PERSONAL SAFETY GOAL → *Make Myself Safe*
by
Regaining Self-control
Calling for Back-Up
Having Someone Else Intervene
Not Intervening

Trying the pause and exhale one more time may be all that is needed to help regain a sense of well-being and self-control.

If the option is available, get someone else to be with you during the intervention. This person's role may vary from witnessing the events to actively engaging in management of the conflict to acting as a decoy for calling you away if the conflict escalates.

Professionals in the human service field use the technique of telling a staff member that they have a phone call. The distraction gives the person an out from the conflict at hand.

Nonprofessionals have mentioned that they might call their friend on the phone before a difficult conversation with a family member. They ask to be called back in ten minutes. The callback serves as a break, allowing people to take a "breather" and maybe even discuss with the friend some options for managing the scene. In highly escalating conflicts, the police are called in for help.

Bowing out of an intervention when someone is more qualified and able to intervene is a reasonable option when you feel unsafe.

Determining your exit plan and adjusting yourself accordingly could provide a measure of safety so that you can continue with the intervention. Feeling literally backed up against a wall during a conflict can be a frightening experience. A small cramped room or many large obstacles blocking your exit to the door can make you feel unsafe even if you are a skilled intervener.

Not getting involved in the conflict in the first place may be the best option when feeling unsafe. However, if another person has targeted you directly, merely walking away may not be an option. In scenarios where you do not feel capable of managing the conflict, intentionally acquiescing to the antagonist may be the only alternative.

When a person is intent on attacking you verbally or physically and you can neither escape the scene nor defend yourself, making a conscious choice to allow the person to continue with their rampage may be the only immediate option. Surrendering the scene or not engaging could mean simply standing still while a person berates you. If you are being physically attacked and are unable to defend yourself, curl up into a ball to protect your organs and face.

I mention the need to make a calculated surrender at times because of stories I have heard about people being critically injured during a physical attack. One form of calculated surrender may involve consciously making a choice to relinquish some level of control to an antagonist. This keeps a thread of scene control in your hands. Although it may seem insignificant and certainly wouldn't lessen the verbal or physical blows of such an attack, it will serve to maintain a sense of self-integrity rather than total surrender.

Summary: Take the Time to Ensure Personal Safety

Regardless of the amount of experience you have, it can be initially disorienting to hear the loud voice of an agitated person. Working long hours, being preoccupied with troubles at home, or simply being overwhelmed with the problem at hand can all contribute to poor decision making and conflict escalation.

The natural "fight-or-flight" response will always be urging you to take a less–than–calculated conflict management approach. Self-leadership is crucial and necessary if you are truly seeking de-escalation.

It takes minimal time to assess whether you are safe. The pause and exhale are done simultaneously and take five seconds.

Despite the apparent simplicity of taking time to pause and exhale, the step will require practice. No need to despair, though. The technique provides an immediate sense of self-empowerment. The pause can allow you to manage conflict instead of being baffled by the task at hand. Your inner sense of well-being will likely become contagious. Those who are caught up in emotional turmoil seek those who are projecting a sense of calm and well-being. Say "Ahhhhh" and exhale, and you will be on the right path.

Is the Scene Safe?

Common sense should advise you to be wary before proceeding into a chaotic scene. Yet many people throw caution to the wind. Anyone who feels immune to getting hit when stepping between two fighters, for instance, may realize in hindsight that sheer luck kept harm away.

A scene that is visibly chaotic, emotionally charged, and potentially volatile is not safe, period, regardless of other factors. Approach such conflicts with calculated caution. Instead of being swept away by the ensuing hysteria of emotions, learn to view a scene objectively.

Let's explore scene safety assessment. Once personal safety is attained, the next step is to appraise the level of safety in the surrounding environment. Like personal safety assessment, this stage is expected to take minimal time.

The Feel, Look, Listen Approach Revisited

A quick review of scene assessment uses the "Feel, Look, Listen" approach.

- Feel: Acknowledge your intuitive sense. What feels safe? What doesn't feel safe?
- Look: Observe the whole scene. Does something or someone seem out of place?
- Listen: Ascertain what is being said. What is the overall timbre of voices in the room?

Throughout an intervention, continue to feel the mood or tension in the room, look for visual indicators, and listen for auditory cues. The following chart demonstrates.

> ### Goal-Oriented Intervention Model
> *"Is the scene safe?"*
> *Feel*
> *Look*
> *Listen*

Make the Scene Safe

An expedient way to secure scene safety is by separating the conflicting parties. Using a verbal prompt to distract two angry people, for instance, is a common technique. "Michael, come on. Let's get out of here and take a break." This prompt may be all that is needed to pull someone out of a conflict.

Depending upon your authority or relationship to those involved in a conflict, the verbal prompt may differ. For instance, like a parent or a teacher, a police officer may use authority to demand instant separation with the expectation that they will be listened to: "Break it up, you two!"

If you are intervening with complete strangers, a more neutral and aligning statement is necessary. Personal safety is of the utmost importance in such a case due to the possibility of personal attack. A verbal prompt such as "Walk with me, please," if done in a sincere and strong tone, has been sufficient at times to separate someone from a conflict.

Removing objects that may hinder movement can help to make a scene safe. Toys on the floor, chairs blocking an exit or movement, and similar large and small objects can be hazards. Moving items to the side or out of the room entirely can set a tone of spaciousness and safety. People are less likely to feel cramped and bothered by a room that allows movement and fewer stimuli.

Containing someone who is volatile is not necessarily done as a physical intervention. Asking or telling a person to take a "time-out" is a widely used technique. Parents may send their child to her room or a safe corner, away from spectators and antagonists. Human service workers use the phrase, "Do you want a time-out?" when directing an angry person to pause and stop certain behaviors. Many educators set aside a space in the classroom for students who need a little quiet time to reflect and regain a sense of self-control.

Spectators incite violence. There are two options available when spectators are involved: you can move away from the onlookers, or you can move the onlookers away. Removing onlookers decreases the tendency for angry parties to perform as if in front of an audience. Again, depending upon your relationship to onlookers, the task may or may not be difficult. As a rule of thumb, spectators will be more willing to move away without question when directed by an authority figure.

People's images precede them when they have a particular role. A teacher, for instance, by virtue of her job, is an authority figure who can act in a positive manner to direct and control an environment that is conducive to learning. The students' expectation is that she will be capable, even before they meet her, because she is in the role of a teacher.

"Never underestimate the amount of authority that you have by virtue of your job and who you are as a person." This is one of my favorite sayings that I bring up during workshops. It has been my experience that people forget that they are looked to as the "one in charge," whether they are at work, at home, or just an adult who happens see a group of youngsters bullying another child. When I say this short phrase, participants slowly shake their heads as if remembering a long forgotten memory. We are all responsible and capable of making our world safe. Authority is not necessarily measured by how loudly you speak nor how many people you command, but by the intent behind your actions.

There is a fine balance between using and abusing the power of authority. By and large, humans are extremely perceptive. We sense when we are being abused, manipulated, or coerced and are less likely to willingly comply. On the other hand, I have notice that when a person assumes a position of authority and speaks with clarity and compassion, most people listen and readily follow that person's directives.

Speaking to the Angry Crowd

The night was pitch dark and the roads were slick with ice as I made my way home one evening after class. About a mile from my house, I noticed a bit of traffic ahead and knew intuitively that there had been an accident. I pulled my car off to the side of the road. I quickly stepped out and slipped, falling flat on my back. With a thud I landed. "Ouch!" I cried out to no one in particular. Carefully and slowly, I rose. I would have to walk at least twenty-five yards to the scene ahead and seriously considered getting into my car and going home. My attention was caught, however, when I heard angry voices and saw someone lying in the middle of the road. "All right," I said to myself. "You're not hurt. Now go forward and see if you can help."

As I approached, I saw a number of men yelling at two other men, one who was sitting in his car and another who was lying on his back in the middle of the road. I recognized these men, but I didn't know any of them personally. I could see that one young man was focused on the person lying on the road. He was saying something like, "I'm gonna teach you a lesson, you drunk. Look at what you two idiots did to my car!" I observed the crowd—none of them was ready to intervene. I felt the timing was right for me to step in out of the dark.

"I'm an EMT. I'll check out this man," I called out. The all-male crowd stepped back as I moved into the slight glow from surrounding headlights. The angry young man said that the guy lying down wasn't worth it. "I have my job to do," I replied. With slow and cautious steps, I moved next to the man lying on the road. He yelled a babble of angry words. Looking down at the shivering man, I said, "I am not the enemy. I am here to help." The surrounding voices grew quiet, and I proceeded to check the man on the road.

In the end, no one was hurt, and only vehicles had been damaged by the slight fender bender. When the police cruiser arrived, I made my exit. Once again, I appreciated the value of taking my time, observing the scene first to ensure my own safety, and speaking with authority and compassion. Stating my position, not getting involved with the conflict, and being a voice of reason were important in that I was able to move the focus of attention away from anger and toward de-escalation.

Another lesson reminded me of the importance of assessing a situation. I can still feel the thud of my own body falling to the ground before I finally decided to intervene. I had carelessly stepped out too soon. Here was a concrete reminder to slow down and assess the scene. If I had assessed the scene before getting out of my car, I would have noticed the black ice and been more careful. Personal safety is of the utmost importance.

It has never ceased to surprise me that people listen when I speak up in a clear and concise fashion during a volatile scene. I have been granted authority by virtue of being the one who steps forward to offer a reasonable option to those in conflict. Violence and nonviolence both stand out, but they send two distinctly different messages. The first is a beacon for chaos, while nonviolence signifies inner calm and control. Such presence sets a tone of leadership and self-control.

And remember, intervention at this stage should only be done if personal safety is secured.

Create an alliance that identifies you as working for the common good of those involved in the conflict. This role requires the ability to project neutrality. You might be scratching your head and thinking, How can you create an alliance while maintaining neutrality? The answer is that you ally yourself with the goal of working for the common good of those involved in the conflict. An intervener maintains this position by avoiding face-to-face confrontations. Standing face-to-face with a person who is angry can make you a target. This is where the mediator's stance comes in.

The first couple of words that are spoken by an intervener set the stage for the rest of the intervention. An important point is to remember that everyone's experience is different, and you should respect possible differences. Avoid using interpretive statements like, "I understand that you are angry." The term "I understand" is a common phrase used by professionals and nonprofessionals when speaking to an upset or angry person. You may want to try to understand how you can help someone who is having difficulty, but can you really understand another person's experience? Even if you had a similar episode in your own life, it is unique to your own experience. This is a subtle concept, yet it is very powerful. Many people don't notice the difference, but if there is a choice for a more refined option, why not try it? Instead of saying "I understand," you could try "I would like to understand." Words are powerful, and this small shift is an opening that signifies a willingness to hear more versus the first statement which could be taken as, "I have heard it all before."

I find that creating an alliance helps me to achieve scene safety quickly because I am working with the group instead of trying to control the group. I first wrote about the following scenario for *Aikido Today Magazine.* It is an actual intervention that demonstrates the use of creating an alliance in order to make a scene safe.

Creating an Alliance at the Campground

It was a Friday afternoon, and I was elated. My friends and I were going camping together for three days. When we arrived at our site, a flurry of activity took place as we quickly set up camp. I was holding up a pole for a large tarp to go over the picnic table when I heard the chilling words, "I am going to kill you." It was then that I saw a twenty-something man who had made the threat while stomping across the campground toward a site that was filled with other young people who were taunting him. One young woman in that group grabbed her crotch in a sexually explicit way as if to say, "You jerk, this is what I think of you."

Across from us where another family was camping, I saw the mother grab her small child as she ran into her tent. I noticed a look of horror in her eyes and recognized her desire to flee. My friends and I stood for a moment, and I decided to act. At least I felt personally safe from harm, since I was not the target of the man's threat. The scene was becoming more and more volatile as threats flew between the group and the angry young man.

I began walking slowly toward the young man and the group of antagonists who had surrounded him. "No fighting here. There are children," I called out in a steady and repetitive fashion. Another woman camper across from me also chimed in, "No fighting." She stopped far away from the group, but I kept on walking toward them with my chant, "No fighting here. There are children."

I felt like the eye of a hurricane as I moved in closer to the group and they parted to let me pass. It became obvious to me that my slow and steady movements and words were impacting the entire group. Perhaps some of the participants were taken by surprise that not everyone was enticed by the potential mob mentality of wanting a fight. Others became curious to see what I was up to and if others would listen. I felt an alliance with those who parted before me and allowed me to go through. No one told me to get lost. The antagonistic group became speechless as I drew closer. I moved up alongside the angry young man and his final target, a man his own age. I had no desire to stand between the two of them and risk being their next target. The two were yelling at each other and threatening to fight. I turned to the young man who had first threatened to kill the other and said, "Walk with me, please."

He turned away, and we stepped together out of the chaos and toward the road. The group again parted and let us out of the circle. The man stopped and turned back for a moment as the crowd teased him about walking away. "Water over the dam," I said, and we kept walking. "You are doing great. Let's keep moving," I encouraged. When we had reached a measurable distance of safety from the group and I no longer felt he would turn back to their taunts, I said, "I would like to hear all about it." The young man's eyes flooded in tears and he began to tell me a story of lost love and hardship as we made our way back to his camp.

I left him at his campsite with a small circle of his own friends and told them to keep him safe. The rest of the weekend was trouble-free. The group of antagonists left soon after my intervention. My new friend and I saw each other across the way from time to time and passed a wave or a nod of the head.

In the situation I just described, with my personal safety intact, I was able to commit myself to making the scene safe. My movements and positioning were calculated to create a presence that posed an opportunity for those too confused by the growing conflict to do anything other than go along with the crowd or to align with me instead. I used concrete phrases that were nonthreatening and truthful. There were children all over the place, and it wasn't the time to fight. I reminded everyone that they could be responsible if they chose to be.

I didn't ask the crowd to move away because their focus was on the angry young man and what he would do next. The area was pretty clear of obstacles, and I wasn't about to move any trees. Getting physical was not my first choice, and that is what I would have had to do to attempt to contain the young men. My only real choice was to try to align with the parties involved, as previously discussed, and show them an alternative to violence. If I had waited until the park ranger appeared, the fight might have already started and ended with someone getting hurt. Asking the young man to walk away gave him and his target an out—a reason to step away.

If the group had not parted and let me through, I would not have gone in to the circle. Since the group did open up quite a bit of space to allow me to pass, I took this as a sign that they accepted my role and were willing to work with me on my terms.

Instead of saying too much, as in, "Hey, you guys, no fighting here. Can't you see that there are children? This is a campground, not a boxing ring," I repeated the same phrase over and over. Not only did my words catch the spectators' attention, but they showed how focused I was on the event. I wasn't acting as one more cog in the wheel. My concentration on the incident made it clear to others that I was in for the duration of the conflict.

Achieving scene safety requires first securing your own personal safety, then reviewing the options available for making the scene safe. Once scene safety is achieved, then you can create an alliance and work with the parties involved toward the goal of helping those in conflict regain a sense of self-control. Options for action are provided in the following chart.

Goal-Oriented Intervention Model
Is the Scene Safe?
SCENE SAFETY   →   *Make the Scene Safe*
GOAL   *by*
Separating Conflicting Parties
Removing Physical Objects
Containing an Angry Person
Moving Away from Spectators
Creating an Alliance

When Personal and Scene Safety Are Not At Risk

If personal safety is not threatened and the scene is safe, options for resolving conflict can be discussed. Everyone involved must be in agreement for working a conflict out, meaning that they will listen and not interrupt others. Until that point, resolution can not be considered. Crisis resolution may happen simultaneously while the scene is being made safe, afterwards when tempers have been quieted, or not at all.

You may initially make an area safe only to find that tempers reheat, and the intervention cannot continue until you again address safety issues. All you can do is keep going back to your initial goal of creating a safe environment, and in the process, keep working toward de-escalation. Having a clear set of questions to ask yourself as you move through the intervention—"Am I safe?" and "Is the scene safe?"—helps to maintain our focus and provides a proactive model for making the scene safe for all. The following examples illustrate this point.

Joan's Overreaction

The halfway house for incarcerated women had been quiet for most of the evening. From her office, Joan could hear the steady murmur of the television down the hall. Louise, the only other staff person on duty, was in the basement helping a resident with her laundry. Joan first heard Helen's voice yell out, "Don't change that channel, girl!"

Chris replied "You're not watching anything. You've got your nose in the magazine!"

Joan jumped out of her chair and ran down the hall. While running down the hall, she yelled out, "Hey, knock it off in there!" Joan took no time to stop at the door and look in. She kept moving until she was next to Chris, who was standing over Helen, her finger pointed in Helen's face. With the background noise of the television, Joan's voice grew louder as she said, "What is going on here? Who was watching first?"

Tamara, Gwen, and Pearl, also in the room, took the opportunity to chime in their own thoughts about who should watch what.

What was Joan's goal: crisis intervention or crisis resolution? Was Joan thinking about safety? How could this intervention be improved?

Joan's was an intervention that attempted to move directly to resolution while bypassing safety. As a result of the ensuing chaos, Joan would now unfortunately have to work even harder, since there were eventually five people involved instead of two. She allowed herself to get off track from what should have been her primary task, which was to ensure personal and scene safety. The program on the television was of little importance. Yet Joan went along with the residents in making it the focal point. Joan's intervention only served to reinforce the explosive model of reacting to conflict with emotionally-guided behavior.

In other words, Joan's intervention was not well considered. Her main goal was to take control in an authoritative manner by demanding the group to "Knock it off in there!" before she even had any idea what was actually going on between Helen and Chris. Joan also risked her own safety by moving directly into the room without assessing the scene. If she had paused at the doorway to take in her surroundings, she might have been able to de-escalate this conflict quickly without risking her safety. Stepping into the middle of the conflict between Helen and Chris was a reactive response on Joan's part and could easily have set her up as the target of the group's anger.

Joan and other interveners who have reacted instead of acting in response to a conflict have done so because they feel that something must be done quickly. Joan was hoping for a quick solution to the problem at hand. She would have been better off, though, being proactive instead of reactive when hoping for a quick solution. Being proactive would have allowed her to stay calm and clearheaded. Not only would Joan have felt in control of herself, but she would have been better able to view the choices available to her for managing the scene, instead of demanding and shouting statements in a threatening manner.

To their end, Tamara, Gwen, and Pearl were doing their part to escalate the conflict. If Joan had paused and at least ad-dressed the other residents by either nodding to signify her control of the scene or by saying, "Could you three please step out of the room?", she would have set up an alliance with them or at least distanced them from the primary conflict. They could ignore her or refuse her request, but at least she would have acknowledged them before moving to Helen and Chris.

Acknowledging the entire scene, not just Helen and Chris, would have shown the rest of the residents that Joan was able to manage multiple tasks and wasn't consumed by the crisis at hand. People want to feel safe. Interveners who project confidence and self-control present a convincing authority and a can-do attitude. People in the middle of crisis are more likely to submit to a person who appears levelheaded than to an intervener who is frantic.

Sally's Intervention

The sky was turquoise on an early December afternoon as Sally walked through the front door of her home on Cleary Street. Before she even took off her overcoat, she heard her oldest daughter, a senior in high school, screaming at her younger sister, "Doris, give me back my shirt!"

Doris came running out into the hallway toward Sally. She had a purple shirt in her hands. Out of the door behind Doris, a plastic cup came flying and hit the wall across the carpeted hall. "I'm going to kill you!" cried Clara. With eyes wide, Doris said to Sally, "She's going crazy again, Mom. This isn't her shirt, and I'm not gonna give it to her!"

Clara walked into the hall with her slipper raised above her head and her other hand clenched into a fist. Upon seeing her mother with Doris, she wailed, "Get away from Mom."

This scenario all happened in less than half a minute. Sally had stepped right into a cross fire of physical threats and verbal assaults. She hadn't done so on purpose. She had been merely returning home from work. The goals of personal safety and scene safety would nevertheless need to prevail.

Sally's first goal should have been safety for herself and her two daughters. It didn't matter whose shirt was whose. Trying to solve that mystery would have to wait until after Doris and Clara had gained control of themselves and could listen, and Clara seemed especially "over the edge." Sally would only escalate the crisis if she tried to converse with the two girls about shirts and ownership. The main concern had to be to make sure that no one got hurt and that threats were not allowed to come to fruition.

Watching the scene unfold, Sally was in a good position to figure out a few possible goals. She needed to pause and exhale in order to think more clearly. She knew there was a risk to safety because Clara had threatened Doris and was holding one hand raised with a potential weapon and the other balled up into a fist. Sally's first goal should have been to separate the two girls so that they could not continue their mutual antagonism. After talking separately with Doris and Clara, Sally might be able to facilitate the two teenagers' coming together to discuss the conflict or ownership of the shirt. Let's see what effect Sally might have on this crisis.

Sally's Intervention Continues

"Doris, I want you to go down the hall and wait for me in my bedroom, please," Sally said.

"Mom!" cried Clara while taking a step closer to her mother "You can't . . . "

Sally cut her oldest daughter off mid-sentence. "Clara, that slipper belongs on the floor and not in the air." Clara slowly brought down her hand with the slipper. Sally continued speaking softly to her daughter. "You are awfully upset. I want to hear from you what has been going on. Let's go into the kitchen. I'll set us up some milk and cookies."

"I don't want any stinking cookies!"

"Okay, but I sure need something, and I would like to sit down and hear your side of the story first."

Doris was sent to her mother's room. Before trying to move Clara out of the hallway, Sally was able to set a clear boundary with her daughter by asking her to put the slipper down. Her soft-spoken style and nurturing manner created an alliance with Clara, or at least reassured Clara that she had not taken sides. If Sally had tried setting a boundary by saying, "Don't you raise your hand to your sister, young lady! Put that arm down! Right now!", no neutrality could be assured. Clara might have continued to move past her mother in order to get to her sister. As it worked out, Sally could now excuse herself for a moment from Clara to check in on Doris. In sum, Sally's take-charge attitude enabled her to set boundaries and helped define her authority as the mother. Her attitude asserted that she would be the one to decide how conflicts were handled and clarified the boundaries and rules.

Making the scene safe often means having to separate two parties in conflict. The separation immediately accomplishes two goals: safety and de-escalation. If there is no one to argue with, an aggressor's anger may be redirected. A time-out will enable parties to rethink ways to work through conflict without getting violent. By taking away the target of someone's anger, you instantly create a safer environment.

De-escalation and safety are often prompted by the mere presence of an authority figure. Each of us has experienced the schoolteacher who can walk into a chaotic classroom and calm everyone solely by her presence or stern look. Parents and direct care staff can use the same nonverbal technique, conveying without a doubt that the dispute must stop. The effectiveness of someone's presence is based on authority and ability to create an alliance, as well as the ability of those in conflict to de-escalate nonviolently.

Knowing Your Personal Boundaries

Making the scene safe and keeping it that way means having a clear sense of personal boundaries, such as how close you allow someone to move toward you or what you feel is appropriate language. Personal boundaries vary depending upon cultural background, ethnicity, family upbringing, and past experiences. Regardless of where boundaries are set, a lack of clear boundaries can make everyone involved feel unsafe.

A scene does not have to be volatile to feel unsafe and threaten boundaries. The next vignette illustrates how easily a boundary can be crossed.

Uncle Jake's Disregard for Personal Boundaries

Uncle Jake's drunk antics at family gatherings were well-known by all. He liked to make loud obnoxious announcements like "Hey, who wants to tease Aunt Jean?" It wasn't unusual for him to start singing lyrics to old songs that would make everyone feel uncomfortable, such as "Driving that train / High on cocaine . . . ," especially in front of the children.

Newcomers to a gathering were typically pulled to the side and forewarned about his behavior. Julienne somehow missed her pre-warning and was taken by surprise when Uncle Jake walked up to her and said, "How about a big hug for me?" and then promptly gave Julienne a big kiss on the lips.

Julienne said later to her boyfriend, who was Uncle Jake's nephew, "I saw him going around the room and doing the same thing to everyone. I knew he was eventually going to make his way to me, and I was going to be prepared. But then he was there, and I just didn't know what to do. I wanted to turn my face away, but I felt frozen. I wish I had just put up my hand and told him to stop. I have never met anyone like him before!"

Julienne could have done exactly what she wished. Everyone is allowed to set her own boundaries. Boundary setting lets the person you are interacting with know what you find permissible for them to do or say to you. You can convey your boundary verbally or nonverbally. To demonstrate, find a partner who will walk toward you from across the room. At some point, the other person begins to enter your personal space. You might say, "Stop!" as they get closer. Nonverbally, your head might retract like a turtle's head going into its shell. People with strong communication skills need only the non-verbal gesture to know that he or she is too close. For people with no concept of personal boundaries, however, clear verbal information is needed for them to realize they have crossed a boundary.

What feels like an acceptable interaction to one person may feel like an intrusion to someone else. Being able to define your own boundaries is as important as paying attention to another person's. Boundary setting can be difficult if you are not used to asking for what you want. An example is, "I hate it when Marsha expects me to hug her each time she sees me. But I feel awkward telling her, like I have a problem with intimacy."

Yolanda's Lesson in Boundary Setting

Every fall, new staff were hired to offset the high turnover of employees at Forest Residential Treatment Center. Unfortunately, the staff development position had been cut from the budget, so orientation to policies and the program was all done on-the-job. Yolanda knew she would be working with adolescents considered adjudicated, placed at Forest by the courts for misdeeds like burglary or assault. She knew she would have to be firm with them. After raising five boys of her own, she felt confident in her skills at working with extreme behaviors. What Yolanda didn't know was how to set boundaries as a direct care staff person working in a therapeutic milieu.

Yolanda's lack of training became evident to her when she asked Henry to wait his turn to use the pay phone. Henry quickly got within inches of Yolanda's face and pointed his finger down at her nose. "I got a right as much as anybody else here to use this phone. You're just new here and don't know the rules yet."

"Well, you may be right, Henry," Yolanda said. "I am new here, but I do know that Chris has two more minutes to use the phone and then it will be your turn." Henry began to respond until he heard the voice of Michele Gordon, the director of the house, yell from behind Yolanda, "Henry! Back away now!"

Later, during a meeting, Yolanda learned the residents were not allowed to approach staff so closely, since most of the residents had a history of violence, possibly including assault. Michele explained to Yolanda that, before any dialogue with an agitated person, she should first ensure her own safety. When Henry was initially approaching Yolanda, she could have raised her hands and asked him to stand back. Since Yolanda didn't stop Henry, who had no concept of respect for boundaries, he kept getting closer to her and disregarded her even more by pointing his finger in her face. Setting limits is as important for the staff member who may be feeling unsafe as it is for the client to see limit-setting modeled. Yolanda was shaken and embarrassed to realize that she had put herself in a potentially dangerous situation.

This scenario and the one with Uncle Jake both illustrate how easy it is for boundary violations to occur. I have often met people like Yolanda who have had close calls when intervening. They become embarrassed by their lack of knowledge and angry with themselves when they realize that their intervention escalated the conflict and put them at risk. "I thought that if I told the patient to move back, I would be infringing upon his rights and that I might get into trouble," said Carla, a new member of the direct care staff at a large psychiatric center for adults. "I was scared when the patient kept coming toward me, but I thought that if I told her to stop or moved away she would think that I didn't care. Maybe she wouldn't stop, and then I didn't know what I would do."

Yolanda and Carla were putting their clients' needs ahead of their own, although their clients would have actually benefitted from explicit boundaries. Another problem arises when the person in crisis doesn't heed your request. This is a valid concern, and it became apparent to me while working on this book. I received a phone call from a mental health agency for adults seeking training in conflict management. When I asked what the specific concerns were, I was told that a worker had recently been attacked by a resident. The worker had been beaten and stabbed by a male resident of the apartment building owned by the agency, which arranges housing for its clients. There is no central data system telling us how many such attacks occur, but in my mind, even one attack is too many.

Perhaps the attack could have been avoided if the woman had received adequate training. At the minimum, she could have learned how to protect herself by knowing how to protect her vital organs and her face by curling up into a ball and, if need be, using self-defense to fight back. Being a caretaker does not mean that you lose the right to self-defense when being attacked. Even if her agency does not allow the use of physical holds for containing a volatile person, she still has the legal right of self-protection. Because she is a human service worker, there is always the risk of litigation if she chooses to defend herself. However, by not protecting herself in the instance described above, she nearly lost her life.

Even minimal training can provide you with an effective level of self-control, which will help you to think clearly and verbalize your boundaries. Modeling a proactive way to speak up for yourself when being overwhelmed by another person is helpful if you are still learning how to set boundaries. Many people have been abused physically, emotionally, or sexually or are just plain shy and are not necessarily skilled at setting limits for themselves. Others simply have no experience in boundary setting.

You Don't Have to be Superhuman!

Having an invincible mind set can also make you unsafe. We will refer to this as the "Superman Complex," implying an overly confident attitude that disregards personal safety. It occurs when you assume an attitude of perfection, of being able to extinguish a conflict with a single word, by leaping into a crisis without hesitation, and of always being "right" in the eyes of others. Don't forget, though. Even Superman has to be safety conscious; Kryptonite could kill him.

Those inclined toward the Superman Complex should remember that to be human is to be imperfect. It can be difficult to accept our imperfections when we hold ourselves up to such high expectations that there is no room for error.

Working through a crisis using problem-solving techniques teaches valuable lessons. For parents, teachers, and human service workers, nothing could be more counterproductive than rushing through a conflict. Such a model only teaches others to develop the same bad habits themselves. Speaking to another person without resorting to an authoritative style, invincible demeanor, or threats is an important model for all to see. It shows that there is no need to resort to greater violence in order to manage a scene. Taking the time needed to work out a crisis is okay and even preferable. It is through the problem-solving process that we learn about others and ourselves.

Set Attainable Goals

What may seem like an attainable goal to one person may seem to another like building a skyscraper. As a child, I played a game called Giant Steps. One person would stand facing away from the group and say "Take one giant step," then "Take three baby steps." The object was to be the first person to tag the speaker so it could be your turn to be in front. Not everyone would get to the speaker at the same time, because everyone's steps were a different size.

This childhood game suggests the difference between what different people see as attainable goals. Problems arise when we put our own expectations on someone else. In the child's game, everyone wanted to take the biggest giant steps. Bigger was better, since it got you that much closer to your goal. Giant steps were the way to go. Baby steps—well, you could take them or leave them. The moral of the story, however, is that small steps are important, too, in attaining your goals. Being first matters only in the game. Persistence and all the little steps can sometimes outweigh any benefit that you may gain by using speed or shortcuts. We must recognize and reward small steps taken by those in conflict.

How does this apply to conflict management? Well, for instance, next time you are intervening in a conflict and you call out to those involved in the conflict by stating their names, "Bonnie," or "Jane," and Bonnie actually turns her head and looks at you, she has just taken a baby step.

Although Bonnie is focused on Jane, her ability to look to the intervener calling her name indicates her recognition of an opportunity to exit the conflict. This small step can and should be acknowledged later by saying something like,

"Bonnie, that was great when you gave me eye contact despite your conflict with Jane. Thank you for not ignoring me." You can even suggest a bigger step for the future: "Next time when you look at me, try taking a step back."

Taking small steps and working toward the goal of making a scene safe instead of taking giant steps like attempting to quickly resolve the conflict with a statement like, "Stop arguing!" simplifies our role as interveners. Turning a negative situation around and pointing out the positive benefits everyone.

Avoid the tendency to view only the negative aspects of a conflict. In the Chinese language the symbol *Ji* (or *Gee*) represents both crisis and opportunity. Redefining a crisis as an opportunity to work on skills of communication and problem-solving takes away the fearful perception of crises as situations to be avoided.

Setting attainable goals helps us to become more effective as interveners. To make the scene safe is an attainable goal, whereas resolving the conflict is not as easily achieved, since conflicting parties do not always want to compromise. When we recognize their importance, baby steps start feeling good and become self-perpetuating.

Superman may be able to leap tall buildings with a single bound, and that is why he is an action hero. We mere mortals can avoid the Superman Complex by appreciating the value of taking little steps. With small steps, we begin to reframe our expectations and feel more at ease. If you are authoritative, you may sometimes be able to take a giant step and quickly resolve a conflict by assuming total control, but a domineering style quickly wears down both you and those in conflict. Instead of just "fixing the problem," effective conflict management means learning how to actively work through a conflict.

Summary: Ensure Personal and Scene Safety

The primary goal of conflict-crisis intervention is to ensure personal and scene safety. The time during conflict escalation is undoubtedly the most dangerous. Conflict management entails addressing safety concerns, whether the dispute is a quarrel between lovers, a fight on the school yard, or an explosive brawl among patrons at a local club. The Goal-Oriented Intervention Model provides a methodical and attainable approach that helps take unknowns out of crisis intervention and makes conflicts safe and manageable.

Aikido's Contribution to Scene Safety

When I was first introduced to Aikido, I was told that if two Aikidoists met each other in battle each would stand waiting for the other to attack. But there are no attacks in Aikido, so the two would wait indefinitely. The concept intrigued me and at the same time felt like a riddle. "Hmmm," I thought. "Would they really stand there forever waiting for the other to attack?"

There is a practice in Aikido of learning to know when the attack will occur. Observing an adversary and learning to sense an imminent attack involves a certain degree of attention to the scene and are part of scene safety assessment. In a similar manner, becoming aware of the scene and being ready with a clear head are important at initial stages of conflict management.

Aikidoists work to perfect a nonviolent approach, including avoidance of inciting violence. The very open stance I described earlier is a powerful tool to this end. During workouts when I have been called upon to attack another student of Aikido, I have had trouble executing a full attack because the person on the receiving end stands in such an open, non-threatening manner. I find I can't muster up the will to make a strong attack.

Finally, Aikidoists work continuously to seek non-reproachful alternatives for meeting violence. Through the practice of Aikido, which takes much skill and a willingness to work for nonviolent solutions, I have learned many valuable lessons about scene safety.

Creating Order

". . . the ultimate weakness of violence is that it is a descending spiral, begetting the very thing it seeks to destroy. Instead of diminishing evil, it multiplies it. . . . Returning violence for violence multiplies violence . . . "

—Martin Luther King, Jr.

If you seek alternatives to meeting violence with violence, you will find a bounty of techniques detailed in this chapter. The goal, once personal and scene safety is ensured, entails helping a person in crisis regain a sense of self-control.

Upholding an attitude of self-assurance and authority is a critical element in the application of any conflict-crisis intervention technique. A successful intervention has as much to do with your command of inner fear as with techniques.

Body language reveals fear in the form of tight shoulders, wide eyes, shaking voice, a flushed or sweating face, and speech like, "Uh, hmmm, well . . . " What then, can be done when your body unexpectedly expresses one of the above fear responses? You can establish order: not external order, like scene safety, but internal order, like getting back into your body.

Men and women alike are pressured to fit into a mold that doesn't quite work for those of us who aren't model material. This constant pressure that many of us face daily to look just so impacts how we feel about our bodies. If you add a bit of stress serum to the equation, like walking into the middle of an explosive conflict, you get people who would like to intervene, but their faces or shoulders are squinched up or held tightly signifying a deeper desire to "get the heck out of the kitchen when the pans are flying."

When surrounded by volatile chaos or facing a threatening person, I think, "Stay in my body." Evidently, I am not alone in feeling uncomfortable: I have worked with many adults who trip over their own feet. A couple have even fallen down as they have lost their balance while trying to figure out how to step away from an agitated person during a role-play, not even a real conflict. I have also seen interveners push other people away when they were frightened and then not remember having done so.

Establish internal order by practicing the pause and exhale. Once you have maintained a normal rate of respiration, address your positioning, or stance. Gaining familiarity with the way you hold your body when intervening decreases the likelihood that you will assume a defensive posture that elicits confrontation.

When I was new to conflict management, I never gave a second thought to how I was standing. I now realize that this often left me vulnerable. Feet squared off, I would take a face-to-face stance. In the direct line of sight, I became the new target for anger. In all, I presented myself as ill-equipped to handle a volatile scene.

The Dangers of an Open Stance in the Emergency Room
While working as a crisis clinician in the ER, I once intervened with a patient who was delusional and fearful. Seeking safety, she tried to lock herself in the bathroom. The head nurse on duty decided to take matters into her own hands and stepped in front of me to speak with the patient. This nurse

had more than twenty-seven years of experience in the ER. Yet her overzealous and poorly thought-out attempt nearly resulted in serious injury.

The nurse stood in an open stance in front of the door while the patient tried to pull the door closed. I happened to catch the door with my foot, which stopped the patient from pulling it shut. If the door had been closed, it would have inadvertently caused the coat hook attached to the door to hit the back of the nurse's head.

During my debriefing with the nurse afterwards, she was astonished to learn how close she had come to being impaled. She had unknowingly put herself at risk because of her unguarded stance. If she had worked with me, her team member, her risk of harm could have been reduced. Instead of stepping between me and the patient, a safer position would have been next to me, situating her out of the direct line of attack and the coat hook.

When you are emotionally involved in a crisis or feeling threatened, it is easy to lose yourself in the conflict. The nurse was oblivious to her face-to-face position. She was vulnerable to physical and verbal harm. An angry person will often vent anger at whoever is in front of her, so keep your body safe: you are the only one who can really do so without having to be rescued by others.

Stay within Sight but Out of Harm's Way

A highly agitated person can lose peripheral vision. The result is tunnel vision. He only sees what is directly in front of him or just off line from the center point of vision. It can be perplexing and downright aggravating when a person doesn't respond to you, even though you are standing side by side, but you are not necessarily being ignored. You are simply out his line of site, which decreases the likelihood that your intervention will be heard. Positioning yourself at a forty-five degree angle in the mediator's stance described earlier helps to ensure that you will be seen and heard without becoming a target yourself. This step is also part of creating an alliance, facilitating discussion instead of confrontation.

With practice, assuming the mediator's stance becomes an automatic response. You will look poised and focused with your body comfortable and relaxed. Those involved in the conflict will be drawn in by your projection of confidence.

"Those involved" in the conflict are the onlookers, antagonists, and scapegoats or targets. You sacrifice your own safety and the opportunity for positive role modeling when you address only the antagonist. Reassuring onlookers with a glance or nod validates scene safety and reinforces the "can-do" image of the intervener. Augmenting your actions with a verbal acknowledgment like "Hi, John," if you already know an onlooker, or just a soft "Hi" to a stranger instills a sense of teamwork and allegiance.

After intervening, I review my positioning, language, and level of focus. Did I set up an alliance? If so, it would be a desired outcome. At any time during my intervention, did I become the target of the other person's anger? If so, of course, it would be an undesired outcome.

I have now become so familiar with the mediator's stance that I naturally stand this way whether or not I am at risk. It is comforting to know that I can stand in a safe position while my mind is trying to manage the fight-or-flight response. If I do need to move quickly, my flexed knees are more likely to move than to lock up and freeze. And in the worst case scenario, my vulnerable body parts are protected from strikes or kicks.

You do not have to be working with a volatile population to appreciate a protective stance and the need to maintain a safe distance when faced with danger. Canoeing among alligators taught me the valuable lesson of respecting others' personal space and providing for an exit.

Everglades

One winter vacation, I went on a seven-day canoeing trip to the Ten Thousand Island section of the Florida Everglades. My friends and I decided to take some of the less traveled routes, which often led us to the resting spots of large, sun-soaked, sleeping alligators. When the current pushed the canoe toward the bank and a gator, we would have to paddle with skill to give a wide berth to the dozing reptile.

Alligators are timid and do not like to be boxed in with no exits. Their huge bodies can whip around in a flash to slide into the water. If you block their escape, you may find yourself capsized in the water with a gator!

Like an alligator, an angry person can flail and should be given a wide berth with plenty of room to move around. There was no need for us to challenge the gator, since it was doing no harm, just as there is no need to block a person if she is not endangering herself or others. The need to leave a scene is the flight side of the fight-or-flight response. Perhaps you can recall leaving a room at one time during an argument. Seeking to flee an uncomfortable scene is not unusual behavior. If a person leaves a scene only to take a break from the conflict, then there is really no reason to stop him from doing so. A time-out serves to give everyone a little breathing room. A break from conflict can be used to reflect on why there is a conflict or what you want to achieve by continuing the debate.

Seeking to flee in order to take a break from conflict is very different than seeking to flee a scene to cause harm. A person who leaves a conflict in order to seek revenge on someone else may need to be physically blocked from doing so. For example, a parent who is mediating a dispute between his two kids might stand in front of one child who threatens to leave the room to find the other and do something unwarranted. You might also need to consider physically stopping a person who, by leaving a conflict, risks harm to anybody. Physically stopping someone does not mean you have to necessarily stand in front of that person. Taking an intoxicated person's car keys is a proactive form of blocking an exit that potentially saves the intoxicated person and others from harm.

Creating Exits: Giving Control Back to the Person in Crisis

As a conflict management technique, creating an exit can be both visible and verbal. You can offer a physical exit by standing in a mediator's stance. The forty-five-degree angle of this stance allows quick departure for either party. Verbal exits may take the form of providing options or asking the person to consider options during a conflict. Open and inclusive statements acknowledge the ability of a person in crisis to think for herself and create an opportunity for a win / win outcome. These two elements unite the person in conflict and the intervener in the quest for reaching a common goal: maintaining or regaining self-control.

The Selective Use of Confrontation as a Management Technique

Confrontation does not provide an exit, nor does it elicit a conciliatory response from a person in conflict. This does not mean, however, that confrontation is ineffective and should never be used. On the contrary under the right circumstances, confrontation can be the quickest and most appropriate intervention. For instance, "John! Sit down now!" is a directive when said with an authoritative intonation that may get John to sit right down. The limitation of this style is that it quickly loses its impact when overused. It is a domineering approach toward problem solving. Confrontation is focused on stopping the behavior rather than helping those involved in the conflict feel safe or gain skills. The win / lose outcome typical of confrontation creates an adversarial dynamic between parties.

Understanding the Roots of Anger and Aggression

Dr. Barry J. Nigrosh's 1983 article, "Physical Contact Skills in Specialized Training for Prevention and Management of Violence," refers to the fear of loss of self-control as a generalized cause of anger or aggression. Dr. Nigrosh says, in essence, that an attack or violent episode gives a brief moment of power and, hence, relief from hoplessness, but the same episode also causes internal anxiety. If you believe, then, that an angry or aggressive person is reacting out of *the fear of loss of self-control*, then the solution is obvious. You should find avenues to help the angry person regain some semblance of control.

Here lies the biggest challenge for interveners: giving control to those in conflict without giving up control of the situation. For an enraged person, gaining self-control at the height of emotional turmoil is no small task. Giving people options puts the ball back in their court and helps them feel empowered.

The following example will illustrate.

Redirecting Sean's Fear of Loss of Self-control

Sean had just arrived at the halfway house for men in transition from jail to the open community. He had to stay there for the next three months and follow all the rules of the home. One of the toughest rules was a 9:00 PM curfew.

After one week, Sean was already testing the curfew. He had gotten off the phone with a friend who told him that his girlfriend was seeing another guy. After hanging up, Sean was ready to head out the door, but it was 9:00 PM. If he left, he would be in violation of the rules and would have to return to jail and finish his sentence there.

Staff were not expected nor authorized to use physical force to stop residents. Marty, the staff person on duty, was in the lounge with the other residents when Sean called out, "Marty, I gotta go."

Marty, the staff person on duty that night, was sitting in the lounge with other residents. Sean called out, "Marty, I gotta go talk with my girl. I'll be back later."

Marty got up from the couch and walked over to the front door of the house while Sean was putting on his jacket. "It's after nine, Sean. Can't you speak with her tomorrow?"

"She's at some guy's house, and if I don't get there tonight, who knows what will happen?" Sean replied.

"Are you going to throw away all your hard work? What else can you do right now?" Marty asked.

"So I go back to jail," Sean replied

"Think about it for a minute, Sean. Right now you can taste freedom, it's so close. I don't think you really want to throw it all away," Marty said. "Come on into the office, Sean. Let's keep talking."

"Man! I can't just let this girl go!"

"This is about you right now, Sean. Being on probation is hard work."

Sean looked at Marty, who continued speaking to Sean about how hard he had worked to earn an early release from jail.

Marty was simultaneously taking care of Sean's self-image and acknowledging his ability to make the right decision. He could have stated, "You know the rules. You leave now, and you're going right back to jail." This statement, while entirely true and to the point, would have provided no initiative or recourse for Sean. If Sean were able to make it through his first obstacle at the halfway house, though, he would have begun the process of learning how to maintain self-control.

Conflict management provides an opportunity to demonstrate proactive problem solving and behavior management techniques. Confrontation, on the other hand, takes the responsibility for self-control away from the person in crisis and puts it all on the intervener. It is a short-term solution to a long-term problem. Initiating opportunities for the person in conflict to attempt to regain self-control is time-consuming and effort-intensive, but the long-term gains are worth the effort. By offering an opportunity to regain self-control, interveners create a relationship—even if momentary—that allows them to become allies instead of adversaries. Thus, the intervener can remain in dialogue with conflicting parties and be a model for non-aggressive techniques.

In the clinical setting, correctional site, or school system, there is explosive behavior every day due to the fear of loss of self-control.

The following examples illustrate this kind of explosive behavior.

A client was talking on the phone to a relative. The relationship between the two was strained, and the client ended the conversation by slamming the receiver down while shouting expletives into the mouthpiece. Later, the client explained that he had been told he wasn't welcome home for the holidays and that had been the cause for his outburst. Unable to control his family's wishes, he lashed out verbally at the relative and physically at the inanimate object, the telephone.

In a correctional facility, an inmate was told that her weekend furlough had been rejected. The inmate responded by standing up, knocking over a chair, and threatening to assault the social worker.

In school, a student threatened to do bodily harm to a teacher when he received an unfavorable report card. The student may actualize his threat by going home and getting a weapon.

Each scenario describes an outburst that can be attributed to feelings of hopelessness and fear of loss of self-control. If a client does not have the skills for channeling his despair or rage, a violent outburst is likely. Alternately, if the client has some skills, he may start to cry or go to his room, reorient himself, and emerge later to discuss the call with staff.

Explosive behavior may occur when a person externalizes anxiety or anger. Sometimes, however, a person will internalize anxiety. A common way to internalize anxiety is to get sick. While the inmate may become explosive or aggressive, she may also manifest her anxiety by getting sick or becoming moody or depressed.

We can look at each scenario and think, "Gee, isn't that going a bit overboard, to get so mad?" Yet many of us have lashed out when confronted with the fear of loss of self-control. One place we can relate to the experience of the fear of loss of self-control is while driving on the highway.

Fran's Bout with Road Rage

The Friday afternoon rush hour was intense as each driver raced home to start the weekend. A Subaru came up behind Fran's van, its high beams repeatedly flashing on and off, reflecting in Fran's mirror and on the back of his neck. Fran cursed at the driver behind him and called out, "Back off! You idiot!" Eventually, the gray Subaru pulled to the right of the van and slithered by while beeping its horn until the Subaru was in front of the van. For the next two miles, Fran pulled up to less than one car length away from the small station wagon and screamed out, "Think you own the highway, ya moron?" and flashed his lights from low to high. "Ha, that'll teach ya," said Fran.

Fran felt powerful and in control as he chased down the other driver. A sense of satisfaction rushed through him as he thought, "I gave it to that son of a bitch."

Risking his own life and his passengers' lives, Fran responded in a way that is typical of a harried driver. The phenomenon is called "road rage." Too many accidents and deaths have occurred when drivers have become territorial and confrontational on the road. At one time or another, many of us have been in Fran's position. Responding to the fear of loss of self-control, we have allowed our emotions to govern our actions. Unbeknownst to Fran, however, the situation actually offered an opportunity to assume total control and transcend road rage. He could have let the Subaru pass and chosen not to be offended by the other driver's urgency. Instead, he felt challenged and threatened and did not see that he would have been both safe and in control had he just pulled over and let the Subaru pass. "Go ahead, friend. Travel safely," he could have thought.

Addressing the Fear of Loss of Self-control

After your personal safety and scene safety are secured, the next goal, as the chart below demonstrates, is to determine "What does the person in conflict need in order to regain a sense of self-control?"

Goal-Oriented Intervention Model	
CONFLICT MANAGEMENT →	Help Those in Conflict Regain
GOAL	a Sense of Self-control

When an intervention goes well I feel safe, and those involved feel safe enough to listen to my suggestions. The following Ten Tips for Re–Directing Conflict invite you, the reader to simplify your intervention style while helping those involved in the conflict regain a sense of well-being and self-control.

Goal-Oriented Intervention Model

CONFLICT MANAGEMENT   →   *Help Those in Conflict Regain*
GOAL   *a Sense of Self-control*

Ten Tips for Re-Directing Conflict

1. Say a Lot by Saying a Little
2. Remember that Silence Works
3. Acknowledge Emotions
4. Take Things One Step at a Time
5. Set the Pace
6. Be Mindful of Words that Escalate
7. Actively Listen
8. Avoid Objectifying Yourself
9. Tell It Like It Is
10. Create Opportunities

Ten Tips for Re-directing Conflict

1. Say a Lot by Saying a Little

At all my workshops on conflict-crisis intervention, participants are given handouts. The handouts have short scenarios like the ones found in this book. The following is a typical scenario that I use at the workshops. It describes a potential conflict between a teacher and a student.

Mrs. Lewis and Matt

Mrs. Lewis walked into the front door of Pine Street High School and headed to the main office. After grabbing a cup of coffee and picking up her mail, she walked to her classroom and found Matt Simon, one of her senior students, standing at her door. "Mrs. Lewis," Matt said "I can't get no D in this class, you know. If I don't get at least a C—man! I am so sick and tired of this stupid place. I can't get a D! Understand?"

Participants in the workshop are asked to read the story and suggest what Mrs. Lewis should say. In every workshop, participants seem to come up with the following choices:

*1 • "Good morning, Matt." *say a lot by paying little* *1

2 • "Let me put down this mail and we can talk about what is bothering you."

3 • "Would you like to step inside the room and speak with me?"

4 • "You'd better lower your voice, young man!"

5 • "I understand that getting a low mark can be pretty disappointing."

The first reply, "Good morning, Matt," is direct. It also sets a norm that says, "I, Mrs. Lewis, am not upset by your swearing and demanding words."

The second reply is a bit wordy. Asking an upset person to wait a minute while you put down your mail is likely to get him even more agitated. It is obvious that Matt has been waiting a while and wants some type of answer right then.

The third response is potentially dangerous. It is safer for the teacher and student to stay in the hallway, at least until Mrs. Lewis catches the attention of another teacher in the hallway. She might nod to the teacher and get some acknowledgment back, ensuring that she and Matt are being monitored.

The fourth response may get Matt to lower his voice, but it also may incite Matt to increase his volume. Matt may very well be expecting to hear something like "Lower your voice, young man," just so that he can continue to target Mrs. Lewis. "This is a low voice. You don't want to hear me get loud, lady," he might say.

The fifth response is what is called an interpretive statement. Interestingly, participants are amazed to discover how often they use interpretive statements like, "I understand that getting a low mark can be pretty disappointing." Another way of expressing compassion and integrating the third principle acknowledging emotions is to reflect the other person's feeling, as in, "You have a lot going on."

There is a tendency to talk on and on with someone who is too upset to hear anything except a few words. After this exercise, participants in workshops are shortly seen correcting each other and noting how antagonistic their interventions can be, when all along they felt that it was the other person who was escalating the incident.

Another response to Matt Simon besides the ones listed is, "I'm glad you came to see me, Matt." This statement speaks to Matt's need to be heard and begins the conversation on a positive note. By complimenting Matt's action, Mrs. Lewis takes the first step of creating a working relationship with this troubled student. It is very unlikely that Matt will target this person who is saying she is glad he came to see her.

Of all the responses, the first—"Good morning, Matt" and "I'm glad you came to see me, Matt"—are good examples of how to say a lot by saying a little. Feeling caught off guard or tongue-twisted during a conflict contributes to wordy replies. Participants get to experience this effect first hand while performing in a workshop role-play which I use to provide real time data for assessing our intervention styles.

Participants are asked to make up their own role-plays, based upon real life experiences. I often ask participants to do the role-play first without giving a thought about how to help the person in crisis. I do so because at times people in the audience will gasp and say, "I saw someone do the same thing yesterday. No wonder that scene escalated." When the same players do the role-play a second time, there is a baseline from which we can decipher the correct way to help a person in conflict. The following role-play illustrates two possible interventions for a secretary at a doctor's office who is managing an agitated patient.

Joan Sunderland and Mr. Woodruff

Mr. Woodruff was tapping his foot on the floor and looking at his watch for the umpteenth time in Doctor Harvey's waiting room. Dr. Harvey's secretaries Joan Sutherland and Marsha Pickett had barely noticed Mr. Woodruff's irritation. However, they were fully aware that the doctor's schedule was off by about an hour.

Mr. Woodruff got up from his seat and stomped over to Joan Sunderland's desk behind a glass window in the reception area.

Joan Sunderland looked up.

"I want to see the doctor now!" Mr. Woodruff said " I have been waiting for over an hour. My wife is at home waiting for me, and she needs me to help her get around. I can't wait any more."

"Well, would you like to reschedule?" Joan Sunderland began.

"That's not what I want, and you know it," replied Mr. Woodruff.

Marsha Pickett, Joan's coworker, overheard the conversation and added her two cents. "This is a doctor's office. Now you pipe down! We will call you when it is your turn. Now either take a seat or please leave the waiting room."

"How dare you?" screamed Mr. Woodruff.

The conflict had begun to escalate. I stopped the role-play and asked the man playing Mr. Woodruff, "What did you hear the secretaries say to you?"

"I didn't hear anything. I could feel that I was going to have to wait longer, and I felt pretty upset about that."

When I ask him what he wanted to hear, he replied, "I was hoping they would help me somehow."

The scene was to be replayed a second time with the secretaries practicing the first principle: Say a lot by saying a little, while working toward the goal of helping Mr. Woodruff to regain a sense of well-being.

They began where Mr. Woodruff got up from his seat and stomped over to Joan Sunderland's reception area.

"I want to see the doctor now!" Mr. Woodruff said. "I have been waiting for over an hour. My wife is at home waiting for me and she needs me to help her get around. I can't wait anymore."

"Well, would you like to reschedule?" Joan Sunderland began.

"I need to see the doctor now," screamed Mr. Woodruff

Marsha Pickett, whose desk was next to Joan Sunderland's, said, "Mr. Woodruff—"

Upon hearing his name, Mr. Woodruff turned his head in her direction and nodded.

"Let me help you over here."

"I want to see the doctor now," Mr. Woodruff said firmly but in a lower tone of voice.

"You have been very inconvenienced, and I am so sorry. The doctor had an emergency this morning, and it has set our office back. You see that woman over there? She is going in right now, and then it will be your turn. Would it help if you called your wife to check in on her?"

"Uh? Yeah. That would be good," he replied.

"Come over to my desk, and you can use this line."

The role-play ended and I asked Mr. Woodruff what he was able to hear this time around. He was able to recall specific examples such as "I heard my name" or "I heard that I was going to be helped."

When people are agitated, it is difficult for them to take in more than a few words from those who are trying to help. If you are the intervener, you should speak using only short sentences or try identifying yourself and calling the agitated person by name. If he is able to acknowledge the contact, he might be able to hear the next intervention. If he does not respond, it may be an indication of a psychotic state of mind, the use of drugs or alcohol, or pure obstinacy. For the brief moment when an agitated person does respond to his name, a connection has been made and the beginnings of an alliance created. The person intervening can continue by acknowledging the alliance: "Thanks for listening" or "I appreciate your attentiveness."

If an agitated person responds to her name by a turn of the head, eye contact, or a gesture such as putting up her hand as if to say, "Don't bother me," the intervener should continue giving brief directives. "Turn away," "Come with me," or "Walk

short sentences (handwritten margin note)

Call by name (handwritten margin note)

with me" are a few examples. The idea is to give clear verbal commands that can be heard and understood. More importantly, the commands should be concrete and attainable.

Concrete commands

2. Remember that Silence Works

From experience, I know that it can be hard to keep quiet, especially when you feel that the other person is in the wrong. Most of us are used to uninhibited, rapid discourse with colleagues, friends, or family. It is challenging to hold back spontaneous reaction. A few seconds of attentive silence can feel like a lifetime during an intervention. However, presenting quiet composure saves time and keeps the intervention focused on safety. Resolution and debriefing can wait until all parties are willing to listen.

Practicing Silence

Quiet time alone at least once a day without the television or radio blaring may seem like a small request, but for many it can be difficult to achieve. In our society, we are used to constant media stimulation. Try muting the television or putting on a music-only radio station or recording. Taking little steps makes the goal of being at peace with silence manageable and attainable.

peace ē silence

Despite persistent attempts to get us riled, I believe a person in crisis is hoping that those who intervene will remain in control.

3. Acknowledge Emotions

Providing an outlet and emotional space for someone who is holding tight to emotions is a small gesture that can guide them into a deeper understanding of how feelings affect actions. You can say, "This must be very hard for you to hear" or "Your lip is quivering. Do you want to cry?" Such leading statements permit the release of emotions. When people are upset or angry, they are vulnerable and can be led into an emotional release more easily than when they have regained their composure.

Some people cry, some yell, and others shake when upset. Holding back and not releasing your emotions only serves to

not releasing emotions leads to more stress.

increase the stress associated with a crisis. Letting out an emotional release in a safe setting, with a friend, a professional intervener, or a counselor can reduce tension and provide a renewed state of self-control.

Permission to Cry

Late one evening, I was called into the emergency room to see a patient who had been described on the phone to me by the nurse as catatonic. I was working as an on-call crisis intervener for the community human resource center. Not even his family had been able to get any response out of the man. Right after I arrived, he rose and walked out of the hospital. I followed him with an officer in a cruiser nearby to make sure the scene stayed safe. If the patient had become combative, or if he had threatened me verbally or physically, the officer could have exited the cruiser and spoken to the man. If necessary, he could have physically controlled the man to keep him safe and me out of harm's way.

The patient's face was grim and his body held stiffly. Walking by his side, I asked, "May I put my hand on your shoulder?"

He nodded his head and began to cry. Once he was able to experience the emotional release, he told me how frustrated he was with having to do his taxes. It was April 14, the night before his tax return was due. He admitted to being overtired, frustrated, and stressed. I listened for a long time. After emoting, he was able to head home and return to his family. He needed some sleep and was able to decide it wasn't such a big deal to file an extension and do his return when he was under less stress. Such emotional release can help people regain self-control.

This man, lip quivering and body rigid, was able to reveal his vulnerability with a safe witness. Given the opportunity, people in pain will receive acts of kindness and release pent-up frustration and stress.

4. Take Things One Step at a Time

Although as the intervener of a conflict you may have your goal set on safety, people in the conflict will be wondering,

"How am I going to solve this problem right now?" People in crisis can be consumed by the quest to find a solution to their situation. The scene may be safe, but your friend, family member or client may still be caught up in the search for resolution.

People in a state of emotional upheaval tend to take on more than they can handle. You can help initiate structure by directing the person to take one step at a time. The first step is always aimed at helping the person regain a sense of self-control. Guiding the person to slow down his or her breathing, such as by saying, "Let's both take a deep breath in and out, slowly" or offering the person a glass of water, provides an immediate focus.

During crisis calls over the telephone, asking a person what he had to eat that day can serve both to distract and to gather information about how well he is taking care of himself. You might also have the person find some crackers and take a few bites while on the phone. Remember that lack of food or high levels of alcohol can contribute to irrational or agitated behavior.

Once a person's physical well-being is addressed, you can begin to identify external factors that will continue to help them regain a sense of self-control. Notice how the statement, "Let's figure out what you can do right now, instead of what you have to do tonight." establishes focus on the immediate scene. As the intervener, you are like a gatekeeper. If you don't maintain a boundary around what should or shouldn't be discussed, then you will have an onslaught of information to manage.

Keeping the Moment in Perspective

During one late-night crisis phone call, I was talking with a woman who was so angry at her husband that she was ready to pack up her clothes and leave with the children. Knowing her history, I was aware that it was not a case of domestic violence. The couple had ongoing miscommunication which often grew into threats about divorce and custody. She wanted to talk about how she was going to leave and get a divorce. I

only take on to do what you can handle

no food & alcohol

keep communication OPEN

asked her instead what she could do right now that would help her and her children get some sleep. When she started to take smaller steps and not discuss what she was going to do with the rest of her life, the problem became more manageable and she regained her self-control. I knew that determining a long-term solution to the woman's conflict with her husband should occur when she was not as emotionally reactive or angry. Once the initial volatility of the conflict had diminished and she had regained a sense of self-control, she might be referred to seek individual counseling, couples counseling, or professional mediation services to discuss plans for the rest of her life.

Leading into Present Time

Directing a person to stay in "present time" is a manageable goal. What he can do immediately, while you are speaking to him, helps to break down what feels like an insurmountable crisis. For the woman on the phone, present time meant leaving her husband in the living room and going into her bedroom to talk with me. I instructed her to get a glass of water and take a few slow breaths. She did so and immediately felt more in control of her emotions. From this new starting point, we were able to discuss that the children needed to take baths and get tucked into bed. She didn't have to speak to her husband, she decided, and she agreed that if she did, she would only get upset again.

Sometimes the person in crisis can figure out what steps are needed to provide immediate relief. The woman that I was speaking with needed to be advised. She was too upset to think clearly. Setting up tangible steps helps those in crisis succeed immediately.

5. Set the Pace

Avoid matching an angry person's level of agitation. You may hear, "Everyone says they want to help, but no one ever does," or "Okay. Are you going to do this for me or what? Come on, hurry up!" You can create an alliance by saying, "I am willing to help. Will you work with me to make it happen?"

The intervener must set the pace. If a person gets agitated again because you are not going fast enough to meet her needs, remember that your objective is to keep the scene safe and to take one step at a time. An agitated person who feels that nothing and no one is helping him will not be helped by others who match his frenetic energy.

The conflict management leader has to maintain self-control. An angry person will take notice of a quiet and professional demeanor and will often follow suit. Whether it is a medical emergency or an emotional crisis, the person in charge is expected to be level headed and confident.

6. Be Mindful of Words that Escalate

One of the most overused phrases that can immediately set you apart from another person is to tell him to "Calm down!" *No.!!!* Not only is the command patronizing, it is often ineffective.

"Calm what?"

"My actions?"

"My words?"

"My voice?"

It is best to tell people exactly what they are doing, such as, "You're talking fast." Providing clear information about what people in crisis are or are not doing gives them something tangible to work with:

"You are breathing really quickly."

"When you are pacing around the room, it is hard for me to listen to you."

Terms like "Stop acting out!", "Relax!", or "Get a grip!", mean little to a person in crisis.

Until a person is no longer agitated, you should keep using words or phrases that encourage self-control.

"You're talking really fast."

"Please slow down." *use*

Pause.

Then repeat the phrase again.

If the person acknowledges you by slowing his speech or getting angry and saying, "Stop saying that!" you know that he is listening. You can move on to your next one liner.

"I want to help you."

"Will you work with me?"

Follow these statements with

"Let's both take a slow breath in."

"We can work this out together."

Leading a person into behaviors that provide instant relief and control is very different from demanding that he act in a manner that makes you comfortable. If the person resists your request, avoid feeling offended. Remain in control of your emotions. Perhaps silence is required for a moment or two. Constant awareness of personal safety and scene safety is definitely required. Securing scene safety may require you to stand back and give the person in crisis breathing room to move around without causing personal harm or harm to others.

Sometimes people are unresponsive to attempts geared toward helping them regain a sense of self-control. Intoxicated people are less inclined to listen. When someone is intoxicated and acting in a dangerous way, perhaps threatening others, the person should be given a lot of room to move around. As a last resort, someone intoxicated may be physically restrained and put into mechanical restraints, like handcuffs. Not just anyone can detain a person. Workers such as professional caretakers within a hospital setting or treatment center who are trained in the use of mechanical restraints and police officers are given authorization to use such devices. Nonprofessionals should not place other people in mechanical restraint. You could severely injure a person by tying them up and compromising their circulation or ability to breathe. There are so many other choices available before you need to consider resorting to physical management techniques.

Remember that you must find your own style so that you gain confidence in your skills. Try practicing the exact words you might use. I have integrated the short phrases introduced in this book into my interventions. You may wish to use a variation of these phrases to suit your own style and personality.

7. Actively Listen

As a communication skill, active listening is invaluable, whether you are managing a conflict or consoling a friend. People like to know that they are being heard. Application of this technique requires attentive listening skills like nodding and maintaining alert eye contact. Encouraging statements such as, "Could you say more?" or "Please go on," or "Take your time. I want to hear what you are saying" let the other person know that she is heard and also provide an opportunity for her to elaborate. In an earlier example, Luke used active listening skills with Mary to find out what was troubling her.

Mary said, "I'm so mad."

Luke provided a lead in to further discussion without being too wordy: "Say more."

His two words implied, "I would like to hear all about what happened, Mary," a wordy statement that was shortened with a simple "Say more."

Escalation occurs when someone feels threatened and shut down. You may inadvertently shut a person down by being long-winded or saying, with a sharp tone, "Speak up. I can't hear you," or "Look at me when I am talking with you," or "Are you sure that is what happened?" or "Is that all you have to say for yourself?"

Once a person feels threatened, he will focus on the threat, rendering him unable to hear anything else. With that said, you can take a more expansive view on the definition of active listening. Listen not only to what the other person is saying but also to your own tone and choice of words.

8. Avoid Objectifying Yourself

You objectify yourself when you make interventions like, "The rules are . . . " or "The program says that . . . " or "In this house we . . . "

A program's philosophy or the house rules of a family home provide parameters that govern the way people are expected to interact with each other. Rules are easy targets because rules have no feelings or personality. A statement like "I hate the rules" is not a personal attack at any one being. A rule can be called every nasty name possible and will never be impacted by such name calling.

Instead of making such a rule statement, you might say, "When I found the dirty dishes in the sink, I felt angry and upset." The receiver of your statement might still say, "I hate you, and I don't care how you feel," but that same person will have to face the repercussion of a nasty response. You might respond to the disagreeable response by getting angry, by looking down or away, or by becoming sad and hurt. The visual impact of seeing that you have been affected by what was said has a greater potential for making an attacker think twice about such direct malicious statements.

Let us look at two different types of corrective statements made by a teacher to a student who is swearing in a classroom. First the teacher will rely solely on the authority of a set of rules as a statement of what is or is not allowed in the classroom.

If a student is swearing at a teacher, how should the teacher intervene? The teacher could say, "You know the rules. No swearing."

Such a straightforward intervention might stop the student, but it is more likely that he or she will continue to test the boundaries of the program.

The teacher could instead say, "I treat you with respect. Please don't swear at me."

You might want to use a different choice of words. I know that sometimes I sound corny, but it has been my experience that such statements catch a person's attention. I believe that it is actually refreshing to hear a request that is heartfelt and honest, as long as the request is authentic. People in crisis can often spot phonies.

Reference to rules of a program or the "house rules" should be made when the person is able and willing to reason with the intervener. Reminders about the rules should not be done when a person is highly agitated and looking for a target on which to vent their anger. Humanize your intervention by saying, "What you are saying feels mean-spirited," or "I am not the enemy. I believe in your goodness."

Use "I" statements when intervening

Think, "What do I want this person to do and why?"

Asking a person to abide by a rule is too general a request. Breaking the rule down into a less generalized statement will be more explicit and direct. For instance, if the house rule says there are to be no loud or threatening statements, try "I want to hear what you are saying, but you are speaking so loudly that I can't." Don't say, "The rules are 'no threats.'" Remember that conflict management is a time to create personal safety and scene safety. Discussing inappropriate behavior is best done once a person is willing and able to work toward resolution.

Personalizing your request helps you avoid becoming "The Program." Of course the other person may ignore the "I" statement, but at least it provides a chance for her to hear how her behavior is directly impacting you.

Working with a Shoplifter

I had a job for a season working at an outdoor clothing store when I was in my twenties. The store was in New Haven, Connecticut, and had a storefront facing out toward a busy sidewalk and main thoroughfare in the city. One day, a young man walked in and took a couple of Gore Tex rain jackets into the dressing room. I had a gut feeling that something wasn't right because of his gruff manner. I called the manager, who came in and watched for trouble with me. The manager and I watched the young man emerge from the dressing room with a Gore Tex jacket stuffed under the his own coat. "Hey, you. This store prosecutes shoplifters," the manager called out to the young man. The manager then said to me, "Call the police." In the next moment, I saw the young man push the manager over into a clothing rack and head out the door. He was gone in a flash, and the manager was pretty shaken up.

By stating, "This store prosecutes shoplifters," the manager had set himself up to become a target. Interestingly, I had been standing right next to the manager but had not been pushed by the young man. He could have pushed me, too, but his focus was on the manager who had become the alienating establishment.

I learned a big lesson that day and knew that I would avoid putting myself in the same situation. Another time, I happened to see another person shoplifting at the same store. I walked up to the girl and said, "I make four dollars and twenty five cents an hour. That shirt you have in your bag is going to set me back a whole day's worth of wages." I recall that the shoplifter looked at me with wide eyes. For a moment, we looked into each other's eyes. Then she reached into her bag, passed me the shirt, and hurried out of the store.

At no time during the intervention did I become the establishment. By speaking about how her actions would impact me directly, I avoided becoming a target and instead made an ally. My statement was certainly heartfelt because I was held accountable for my inventory. Regardless of whether or not I would have to pay the store for her theft wasn't the point. I wasn't going to get into a wrestling match over a shirt after seeing the manager get shoved by the last person caught stealing in the store. Personal safety was my priority, but the least I could do then was to let her know that someone other than the establishment would be affected by her theft. Her change of heart became a win / win situation for the two of us.

9. Tell It Like It Is

It is a natural tendency for humans to strive to understand the significance of another's behavior. Such a clinical approach, though, can cause you to overlook the obvious. The following example illustrates this point.

Redirecting Darren's Threat

A workshop participant asked to review an intervention she had with a client.

"I was in my office meeting with Darren, who was acting as if everyone in the building were at fault for his problems. I was left speechless when he said, "You people drive me crazy. You: you are always nagging me. You remind me of my aunt. I feel like smacking you in the face."

I asked the workshop participant what she said to this assault.

"I said, 'What is it about me that reminds you of your aunt?'"

She went on to tell us that Darren started to tell her all the ways that she, his aunt, and his mother had made life miserable for him.

She said she felt safe only when a supervisor came into the office and was able to distract Darren.

This intervener was looking at every possible reason why Darren had made the threat. "Hmm," she seemed to have thought, "Maybe he had some prior problems with his aunt. How can I look like his aunt? We are not the same age."

I told her to take what Darren had said at face value and give him a direct reply.

"I am not your aunt, and I do not want you to hit me."

Stating that you do not want someone to hit you may sound like a weak statement. But stating directly that you do not want to be hit is different from quivering and pleading not to be hit.

When I asked the rest of the workshop participants what was the one thing they all thought when they heard Darren say that he wanted to hit this woman, they all agreed that they were thinking, "Gee, I hope he doesn't hit her." If it had been they that Darren had threatened, they also would have feared for their own safety.

In other words, when faced with a bizarre statement, don't overanalyze. Take it at face value. Decide what it is that you do or don't want an agitated person to do, and then state your side. You can also follow through by saying, "I am here to help you. Let's talk about ways we can work together." Such a statement forms a working alliance which an intervener and a person in crisis can use to move on from the bizarre comment.

Darren had made a very real threat. When the worker did not call him on it, she was overlooking an important indicator of potential danger.

10. Create Opportunities

When I think about creating opportunities, I think about an event that I never thought happen: the fall of the Berlin Wall which had separated East Germany from West Germany from 1961 to 1989. Like many people who had grown up during the Cold War, I never expected the Berlin Wall would be taken down. I certainly did not expect the wall to come down in the peaceful, celebratory way that it did beginning on November 9, 1989. Miracles do happen, given the opportunity.

Not anticipating the possibility of positive change can result in unimpressive outcomes or, worse, self-fulfilling prophecies. Statements like, "That child has been kicked out of every school system in the country. I wish you a lot of luck come September. You are going to need it," or, "Dad is never going to change. He never listens to my side of the story and he never will," perpetuate a sense of failure for all. When a person hears statements about himself like, "Here comes trouble with a capital T," being "bad" becomes part of his persona regardless of his present behavior. Changing a reputation is hard enough to do, but it becomes nearly impossible when everyone surrounding him expects failure. Instead, you should create an opportunity for a ray of hope that people can change for the better.

Being non-judgmental and optimistic does not mean that you are a pushover. On the contrary, such traits are proactive. Believing in a person's potential despite her history is a trait of an effective intervener. Healing and change do happen, given the opportunity.

Redirecting Michael toward a New Goal

Michael was young, fearless, and obstinate toward authority. He was in a short-term treatment setting where I was a staff member. Michael seemed to have an unwavering goal to get me angry or embarrass me. I was sure he spent every waking hour thinking of ways to get me upset.

Instead of correcting him, I decided to do exactly what he didn't expect. I leveled with him. I asked him into my office and told him that he was doing a great job of getting me going, day in and day out. We could continue like this until he left the program, I told him, but I had a job to do. I said, "I think you are smarter than that, and I'm hoping that you are wanting to wave good-bye to this place and are going to become a positive leader for this group. You are a natural leader, but you have to choose which way you are going to go. You can waste your time here or you can take control of your life."

Michael looked dumbfounded and didn't reply. Later that day, though, I noticed that Michael had changed. He began speaking up to other group members who were horse-playing and disrespecting staff. I vividly recall breathing a sigh of relief, both for Michael and myself. He had certainly been "getting my goat," an exhausting experience that benefits no one.

I also made an important change that morning by embracing the concept of "create opportunities." It is hard to keep the faith when you have to manage angry and aggressive people. It is easy to become cynical, consumed, and emotionally depleted. Our conflict changed the moment I chose to reorient my judgment of Michael. Instead of seeing him as a nuisance, I was able to rise above that limited view and offer the opportunity for him to channel his behavior in a way that rewarded him. Aggression can be reshaped into the positive attribute of assertion, if you provide appropriate direction and leadership.

offer choices

change negative into positive

Summary

Refining your technique and trying new approaches are scary and take courage. Be patient with yourself. The Goal-Oriented Intervention Model will help transform what appears to be a complex problem into a simple, step-by-step conflict management procedure.

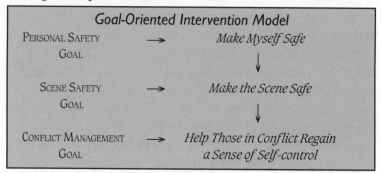

Once personal safety is secured, multiple options for redirecting conflict will come to light. The Ten Tips for Redirecting Conflict provide a resource of options for addressing the conflict management goal of helping those in conflict regain a sense of self-control. Instead of feeling overwhelmed by conflict, you become enticed to create opportunities for change.

Don't Forget to Breathe

There is a sound of ah-ing in the woods. You hear it and know a storm is nigh, and every tree knows it, and every waving branch.

—John Muir

In the snow-laden hills of western Massachusetts, in the mountains of British Columbia, and surrounded by the eucalyptus forest of Santa Cruz, I have breathed deeply. And I have never forgotten the smell of that fragrant air.

In my yard, surrounding the driveway, stand tall Eastern White Pines. Even the subtlest wind will make trees sing "Whoosh!" Having lived in a forest landscape for some time now, I have come to rely on the pines each time I come home from a business trip or long day away. The formidable trees sway above me, enticing me to sigh and take in fresh air.

The influence of breath during a conflict-crisis is fascinating. This chapter explores the effect of breath throughout an intervention. Although we all breathe, not all of us exercise the full potential of purposeful breathing during conflict-crisis intervention.

The involuntary nature of the respiratory system allows us to work, play, and sleep without having to give a thought to breathing. In each twenty-four hour cycle, a healthy adult takes approximately seventeen thousand breaths. Breathing happens, even if we choose temporarily to hold our breath, slow it down, or quicken the rate.

The respiratory system is paradoxical. There is an apparent contradiction in the ability to be voluntary and involuntary at the same time. I remember my childhood effort to test this contradiction, holding my breath until my involuntary system took over, forcing an exhale with a loud puff. My innocent analytical mind was both challenged and perplexed by this physiological enigma.

Martial arts, the practice of yoga, and many exercise programs teach breathing techniques. Professional athletes use breathing as a way of maintaining focus while staying relaxed. Notice the basketball player preparing to take a foul shot and the pitcher readying for a throw. They always pause and breathe to focus the moment. Deliberate use of breathing techniques elevates breathing from an automatic function to a meditative form of self-control. Managing our breathing during a crisis and helping others regain control of respiration are part of the crisis intervener's role.

How We Breathe

Our lungs extend from the top of the shoulders all the way down to the base of the rib cage. Breathing that expands the belly along with the chest is known as abdominal breathing. Quality abdominal breaths are deliberate, requiring slow intake and full expansion.

Short, gulping breathing that raises only the upper chest cavity is known as chest breathing. This type of breathing requires that the involuntary system take over when we need to expel carbon dioxide. The brain, which is the command center for vital functions, maintains bodily function by coordinating adequate oxygen intake and carbon dioxide expulsion. Through an occasional yawn or sigh, we relieve tension and expel carbon dioxide.

Emotions strongly influence the rate of respiration. In his book *Conscious Breathing* (1995), Gay Hendricks writes about the fight-or-flight response and how it affects our breathing: "Belly muscles tighten, our breath shifts up into the chest, and our breathing speeds up. We are poised to run or fight back." Hendricks also notes the capacity to take charge of our breathing: "Human consciousness is powerful enough that we can notice when we are in a stressed breathing pattern and do something about it. We can consciously take deeper, slower breaths, and we can consciously shift our breathing from chest to belly."

Intervening and Breathing

Two of my summers during college were spent lifeguarding at Indian Wells State Park on the Housatonic River in Connecticut. Sitting on a ten-foot tall white chair, I was in full view of the entire beach. Whenever I stood up, blew the whistle, or jumped off my perch, it seemed that the entire waterfront would watch in anticipation of a rescue.

Lifeguards are expected by the general public to perform their duties in an exemplary manner. I likely disappointed a few people on the beach in 1979 when, running with a tank of oxygen to the scene of a rescue, I fell flat on the ground on my face. I had no choice except to get myself up and keep running. But the wind had been knocked out of my lungs, and each step I took became a Herculean feat.

From behind me, as I moved slowly down the beach, I heard the familiar voice of one of my lifeguard team members say, "I'll take the tank." I quickly passed the oxygen to him, and off he ran down the shore to the scene of the rescue. I stood for a moment and slowed my breathing down. Once my breathing slowed, I was able to set off running with little effort. At the scene I found that the swimmer had been quickly rescued by my team members. The swimmer was sitting on the beach upon one of our wool blankets and breathing normally. I thanked the guard who had taken the tank for helping me out and then headed back to my post.

When performing a rescue, a lifeguard's oxygen supply is vulnerable and is never to be taken for granted. A drowning swimmer is desperate and hysterical. Given the chance, he will flail at, climb upon, and push a rescuer underwater. Water rescuers are an extreme illustration of crisis interveners who are necessarily acutely aware of the importance of maintaining a steady flow of oxygen. However, when it comes to needing oxygen to function, the human brain doesn't differentiate between full-time professional and nonprofessional emergency workers.

Direct care staff, teachers, nurses, parents, and other nonaquatic conflict managers frequently disregard breathing techniques as superfluous when managing a crisis. "I want to know what to say. I don't have time to think about my breathing" is a common statement by participants of my crisis intervention seminars. "Breathing is, after all, second nature."

Given that so many groups I have worked with consider breathing control to be unimportant, I started to facilitate a structured exercise focusing on breath. Each participant is asked to stand and state name and job title. As we go around the room, the pace quickens. Instead of waiting to stand and then speak, most participants introduce themselves while they are rising out of their chair. Some people's voices are shaky, other people look flushed, and even more are speaking so rapidly that it is hard to hear exactly what they are saying. Some people are asked to repeat their names and titles.

Although everyone knows exactly "what to say," most flounder during the mini crisis commonly known as "The Fear of Public Speaking." Most speakers look nervous and fail to project confidence.

I ask the group to try the same exercise again. This time, they are directed to stand and focus on their breathing by exhaling before saying a word. Once again, a few people begin speaking before they have stood upright. Overall, though, group members are more in command of themselves. Instead of stumbling over words or rushing to finish, participants take their time and speak in an even cadence. Rather than feeling embarrassed for the uncomfortable speakers, the audience is able to relax and really listen.

Like any audience, people in crisis are sensitive to what key players are projecting. They will quickly lose confidence and may even provoke interveners who fail to maintain professional composure during a conflict. What we convey through our stance is often more defining than our words. A normal rate of respiration using abdominal breathing relaxes the body. Besides relaxing the body, purposeful breathing enhances the brain's capacity for critical decision making and problem solving. Seminar participants appear stiff and nervous when they don't take time to focus on their breathing. Interveners who employ breathing techniques find themselves in an open posture that is conducive for creating an alliance with those in conflict.

Breathing as an Indicator

A person in crisis also needs to regain a normal rate of respiration. Agitation, breath holding, and speaking quickly suppress the supply of oxygen. Such a stressed state compromises people's ability to hear even the most effective interventions. The following vignette illustrates how an intervenor who fails to notice a breathing indicator has difficulty helping a person in crisis regain self-control.

Ken Jones scowled, and his chest was heaving up and down. He had just been sent to the office of the vice-principal, Jane Crown, after his homeroom teacher had found him in the hallway of the high school arguing with his girlfriend. "Mister Jones," Mrs. Crown began, "this is twice in one week that you have made an appearance at my office. This is not going to look good on your record this term, and I do plan on speaking with your parents. I knew your older sister Kimberly, who was the valedictorian of her class. Mister Jones, are you listening to me?"

Ken was staring out the window behind Mrs. Crown. "Mister Jones!" Mrs. Crown repeated. He looked up at her. "Did you hear one word that I just said?" demanded Mrs. Crown.

Ken looked blankly at the vice-principal and said, "What?"

The vice-principal's intervention is a classic example of an intervener who unknowingly sabotages her own intervention. A short and concise statement is best when speaking to an agitated person. Mrs. Crown's long winded lecture was too much for Ken to hear. Her reference to Ken's sister Kimberly was self-serving and served only to complicate her intervention.

Let's give Mrs. Crown another chance. This time, she will be more attentive to Ken's fidgeting and his abnormally heavy breathing.

Ken Jones scowled, and his chest was heaving up and down. He had just been sent to the office of the vice-principal, Jane Crown, after his homeroom teacher had found him in the hallway of the high school arguing with his girlfriend. "Ken," Mrs. Crown began, "you're breathing fast!" The vice-principal then took a purposefully loud inhale and slowly exhaled, "Slooow breaths," she said in a low voice. Ken shook his head a bit and turned to look at her. "That's it. Let's work on our breathing first. Okay?" She had clearly caught Ken's attention. He was looking at her in a quizzical manner while breathing deeply through his nose. "Easy, buddy," she said, "our breath can be a good friend when the world feels like it is spinning way too fast."

Conflict management is all about focusing in on a single moment. Mrs. Crown concentrated on Ken's breathing pattern, which is exactly what he needed in order to regain a sense of self-control. One-word or two-word statements are easier for a person in distress to hear than long, drawn out statements. Short phrases like, "Breathing fast?" don't need to be grammatically correct. As Mrs. Crown began to feel that Ken was becoming calmer, her statements grew longer but stayed on task. Her compassionate style of gently guiding the student toward a normal rate of respiration was conducive for building a connection with Ken. He might still be unwilling to discuss the details of his dispute with his girlfriend; regardless, Mrs.

Crown has demonstrated and led Ken through an important exercise that he might be able to use again on his own.

The vice-principal would now be able to discuss the importance of breathing and its use during conflict. The following dialogue might direct Ken to rethink how he manages conflict.

Mrs. Crown could begin with, "When you came into this office you were breathing so fast, you couldn't hear one word that I was saying. Remember?"

Whether or not the student agreed verbally with a "Yes, I remember" or with a nod of the head to designate agreement would not be important. As long as he was breathing normally, her words would be heard. Pushing him to agree with the obvious, that yes, indeed, he was breathing fast and couldn't hear one word she was saying, would serve only to distract him from the overall lesson of this meeting. For instance, he might think, "If I agree to this statement does it mean I am agreeing that I should be punished for my behavior or that I was in the wrong?" Until he was able to get a sense of where the vice-principal was going with her line of reasoning, Ken might wait for her full statement before agreeing to anything. She would need to continue with something like, "Ken, I have learned that if a person isn't breathing normally, they will have a hard time focusing on what another person is saying. I made a couple of statements that helped you refocus on your breathing. What might you be able to do next time you are in a heated argument with another person? Or, how could you help someone who is upset and breathing rapidly?"

Mrs. Crown could now wait for a reply. Because the student wasn't being berated for his behavior, but was being asked for his insight on how to help another person, he would be more likely to be willing to speak up and discuss alternatives to getting upset and angry. If Ken replied with, "I can help them slow down their breathing," the vice-principal could then lead the conversation toward discussing the dispute he had been engaged in before he was sent to the office. Not only would Mrs. Crown have created an alliance, but she would have empowered Ken to think for himself and shown him that she valued his thoughts on such matters.

Even if Ken refused to reply to her request, he would now be in control of his breathing. Whether he wanted to acknowledge that his slowed breathing pattern was better than his prior breathing would not make or break this intervention. The primary goal, to get a person in crisis in control of themselves, had been achieved. Expecting a person to become conversational is too high of an expectation for some people. It takes time to build trust. Regardless, Mrs. Crown made a small victory. She could follow up with Ken again and meet with him to show concern for his well-being and acknowledge just how well he could do something when he set his mind to task.

I was twenty-one years old and had no direct care experience when I first started working in a treatment facility. Luckily, I was assigned to work with John F. Stephen, a man who had both experience and an innate ability to thwart conflicts before they became unmanageable.

John was proactive in his intervention style. His continual observations kept him one step ahead of the group. I enjoyed watching him greet clients as they entered the room for group session. He didn't say something to everyone, but if he saw someone who looked pensive and distracted, he might say something off the cuff and nonsensical, like, "Do you like orange juice?" or "Purple Haze." Usually, the client would make some reply by giggling, pulling back, or smirking. John just stood there cool as a cucumber, with eyes on the client and an ever-present toothpick held to one side of his mouth.

When a person responded to John by saying, "What are you talking about, man?" John would reply, "Glad you could make it today."

As I watched the clients John had singled out enter the room and take a seat, I noticed that two things occurred. They would look around to see if anyone had noticed their interaction with John, and then their bodies would relax. The question served to distract clients and let them know that John had noticed them. John didn't wait until an individual had become immersed in anger. At the first sign of a client's discomfort—held breath, shoulders hunched or eyes down—he made an intervention.

The ability to notice breathing as an indicator of emotional state requires a keen sense of how you breathe yourself. John's ever-present toothpick was part of his regime to quit smoking. It humanized him by demonstrating that he was familiar with stress. It seemed logical, therefore, that he had the ability to see it in others.

There are many breathing indicators. A fearful person might make a wheezing sound, hold his breath, or hyperventilate. Flared nostrils and forceful breathing are signs of frustration. Loud sighing or hisses are obvious indications of irritability or fear. By noticing variations in breathing and other outward indicators like clenched fists or a flushed and sweaty face, you can make a quick analysis of a person's probable state of mind.

Through observation, you can train yourself to see breathing as an indicator of emotion. There are many opportunities, from crowded express lines to family reunions, to observe how people's breathing matches their physical or emotional state.

Next time you are waiting in the checkout line in the grocery store, watch the breathing patterns of the other patrons or cashier. It might look something like the scenario described below.

Forceful Breathing

Holly and Tomas stopped at the supermarket to pick up some necessities. They were going to the 7:30 movie and knew that the store would be closed before the movie finished. It was 7:15; they had fifteen minutes to make it on time. They moved efficiently through the store. They were doing well until they reach the express line.

In front of them were Mrs. Harris and her two daughters, picking up a few extra items for their Sunday dinner with relatives. As Mrs. Harris and her family meandered up to the aisle, putting their items meticulously on the conveyor belt, Holly and Tomas began shifting from one foot to another, both thinking, "We'll make it. She has only eight items." When Mrs. Harris took out her checkbook and began writing in her elegant script, Tomas began to sigh. "How long does it take for someone to write a check?" he whispered loud enough for Holly, the cashier, and the rest of the customers in the line to hear. Holly looked up nervously at Tomas and then at the customers behind him who quickly shifted their eyes and looked away. Everyone held their breath except for Tomas, who was snorting like a bull while thinking about missing his favorite part, the coming attractions. When Mrs. Harris and her two girls finally completed their transaction, the line sighed in unison. Holly and Tomas shoved their items to the cashier, who hurriedly checked them out.

Tomas conveyed his dissatisfaction through his exaggerated breathing. Like a canine's growl, his breathing was powerful and impacted those around him.

A Withheld Breath at a Family Gathering

Lucille and her two sisters, Helen and Maggie, sat around the kitchen table after finishing the dishes and putting away the food from Thanksgiving dinner. A few other relatives sat with them, having coffee. The mood was light and conversation was easy. When Maggie began talking about the upcoming birth of her third grandchild, Helen got up and walked to the sink. Lucille, the oldest of the three sisters, knew that Helen had a hard time listening to the story since Helen's daughter and son-in-law had had too many miscarriages to mention. Lucille walked over to Helen and put her arm around her younger sister, who had barely taken in a breath of air since standing up. Maggie, realizing her mistake, let out a quiet sigh and slowly shook her head. Timothy Junior, five-years-old, said loudly, "What's wrong, everybody?"

Even as children, we begin to notice changes in breathing that occur when family members have disagreements or share in the joy of birth or loss of a loved one. Learning to recognize breathing as an indicator of emotion isn't a new concept. We simply need to fine-tune old skills and use them during interventions.

Commanding Another to Exhale

Kate, on hall duty at the junior high, heard a loud and angry voice from the main stairwell and quickly headed in the direction of the noise. She saw two familiar students standing only a few feet apart. Jeff's nostrils flared, and his face was flushed. The other boy looked frightened and was cowering against the wall. Kate entered the large stairwell and saw clearly that Jeff was holding his air in, his chest puffed up. Aware of her own safety, she moved into Jeff's line of vision, about four feet away, and said, "Exhale, Jeff. Exhale!" Then she puffed up her cheeks and released an explosion of air. The air rushed from Jeff's nose and mouth. Before he could say anything, Kate said, "That's great, Jeff. Now, how about inhaling, too?"

Kate understood that in order to direct Jeff, she would first have to help him gain control of his breathing. It also caused a distraction, since "Exhale, Jeff. Exhale!" wasn't what Jeff expected anyone to say to him. When Kate exhaled, it was hard for Jeff not to join in, since he was holding his breath and his brain was likely begging for him to breathe again.

As a rule, you should be sure that the other person is capable of hearing the intervention. Often, irregular respiration can be due to state of mind and can affect the ability to think clearly. As mentioned before, peripheral vision may be diminished. Instead of saying a lot of words to this person, you should lead him first into a more controlled breathing pattern. If a person regains a regular rhythm, he often becomes less agitated, and he may be able to manage the conflict on his own.

Here are two ways to lead a person back to a normal breathing pattern, guided breathing and paced breathing.

Guided Breathing

Guided breathing is like sharing a yawn. We have all experienced the chain reaction sparked by someone else's yawn. If I verbally draw attention to my breathing when intervening, the other person becomes aware of my respiration and is likely to attend to his own breathing. When I demonstrate a deep, slow breath, he may be inclined to follow along. During an intervention, it is just as important for the intervener as for the person in crisis to be breathing slowly and fully. Avoid saying, "You need to take a deep breath." Such a patronizing statement may only inspire resistance. A less confrontational approach would be to say, "Let's both take a deep breath." The person being spoken to has been respectfully offered a direction and opportunity for control.

This technique can also be used with someone who is agitated and talking fast when you say, "I want to hear you, but you are talking so fast that I can't. Let's both take a deep breath." If the person continues talking, take a couple of slow purposeful deep breaths with the chest rising and falling each time. If the person asks, "What are you doing?" Your reply could be, "I am hoping you will slow your breathing, so we can work together."

Too Enticing to Refuse

I learned the following technique from a naturopathic doctor. I was in my early twenties and had made an appointment with him to get information about some intense abdominal cramps I had recently had. A few days before, I had gone to the emergency room and was told that I might have an ulcer, although the ER doctor was not really certain and had recommended that I go see my regular doctor. As I walked into his office, the first thing he did was take a slim glass carafe filled with crystal clear water from a rack. Attached to the rack was a clear eight ounce water glass. As he poured the pure, cool water from the vase into the glass, my mouth began to water. He asked calmly, "So, how much water have you been drinking lately?"

I nearly climbed across the desk for the glass. Though that happened almost twenty years ago, I will never forget the power of his nonverbal suggestion. By the way, I also did not have an ulcer. I was dehydrated.

Like a fine glass of water, breathing is something to be savored. The doctor easily enticed me to drink more water. Similarly, you can encourage a person in crisis to become aware of his or her breathing by purposefully modeling deliberate inhalations and exhalations.

Paced Breathing

Try accelerating your breathing to the rapid pace of a person in crisis. Then, slowly decelerate your breathing. The person might look at you as if to say, "What is your problem?" It is both a reminder and a distraction to tell her, quite matter-of-factly, that you are breathing at the same rate that she is. It encourages her to shift her focus to her respiration.

The following story illustrates another way of lowering the rate of respiration through a paced breathing count.

Helping Phyllis Regain Control of Her Breathing

On the morning of the training program called "Working with Survivors of Sexual Abuse," I noted that Phyllis was nervous. I could tell, I thought, by her continual shifting body and downward face. During the workshop, she was quiet and removed from the group discussions. I noticed Phyllis's flushed face and clenched hands. When evaluations were being handed in, another participant asked me to see Phyllis, who was in the back room. She was trembling when I entered. I had a strong sense that the workshop had triggered her emotions in some way. I offered my assistance. She said she couldn't drive home because she was so shaky.

She allowed me to take her pulse. It was very rapid. Her breath was shallow and her face was red. I asked her to breathe with me for a minute. To a count of three, we both inhaled. We held our breath for a count of four and then breathed out for a count of three. I increased the count to five, then six. At the same time, I asked her to hold on to the table in front of us and feel the texture of the old oak. As Phyllis focused on her breathing and the tactile stimulation of the table, her trembling went away and her pulse rate decreased.

The exercise that I used with Phyllis was tangible and accessible. At first she felt unable to control both her emotions and her body. By intentionally taking control of her respirations, she took the first step toward gaining back her self-control.

Asking her to hold on to the table brought Phyllis into present time. This particular technique works well when counseling someone whom is scared, angry, or delusional. Having a concrete, tactile focus brings the person's thoughts to the present. You can use a table, the carpet, or the floor—anything concrete.

Counseling on the Phone

Crisis clinicians who counsel people over the phone use techniques like "present time" to help soothe a client. The clinician may ask the client to sit down and then describe the chair that she is sitting in. Is it wood, or is it upholstered? The clinician may then repeat the client's descriptive words, "You are sitting in your kitchen, in that comfy arm chair that you keep by the phone on the wall."

Simple questions that a caller can answer provide attainable goals that are like stepping-stones across a stream. If the stones are too far apart, the caller may not attempt to cross. Evenly spaced stones, like accessible questions that provide the caller with instant success, can be used as a foundation for the rest of the conversation. For instance, if the person begins to get agitated while explaining the reason for the call, you could mention the emotional control displayed a moment ago.

Preliminary questions like finding out if he has eaten or taken medication also serve to provide important baseline information. When counseling a client, family member, or friend on the phone, the goal is to make sure that he feels safe from harm and is capable of taking care of himself. If he is unable to feed himself, he is clearly in need of a face-to-face interview or home visit and referral to a hospital. In-depth analysis should take place only in person.

Over the Phone Breathing Exercise

Once the initial introductory questions are done, you ask the person if she would like to do a breathing exercise. Before you start the exercise, have the person sit. A seated position is more conducive to relaxation than standing. Ask the person to try breathing in through the nose and out through the mouth and to do so while you count for them. This style of breathing helps a person in crisis control the inhalations and exhalations of air. If you fail to give directions on how to breathe, some people may do the entire exercise while breathing through the mouth Mouth breathing leads to a shallower, gasping style of inhalation and exhalation and is not desirable.

Begin with, "Inhale. One, one-thousand; two, one-thousand; three, one-thousand; four, one-thousand. And hold your breath. One, one-thousand; two, one-thousand; three, one-thousand; four, one-thousand. And exhale. One, one-thousand; two, one-thousand; three, one-thousand; four, one-thousand."

Saying something like "You are sitting in your kitchen, in that yellow chair by the window" directs a person in distress into present time, reduces anxiety, and helps her regain a normal breathing pattern. Once this is accomplished, you can begin discussing the reason she called. If you attempt to discuss her crisis without first getting the caller into present time, it will be difficult to discern if the caller is really able to hear what you are saying.

Callers to emergency lines are often anxious and, as a result, their breathing is labored. A dispatcher can hear the struggle as a caller inhales with a wheeze. Emergency dispatchers nevertheless need to get information. If the caller is completely unable to speak due to his failed attempts to breathe, the dispatcher may ask the person to take a slow breath in and exhale, and then ask him for the information again. "Sir. Take a big breath in and exhale slowly. Good. Now what is the name of the street where you saw the car accident?"

You can do the following stress exercise yourself, or you can facilitate for others through this calming technique. The goal of the exercise is to guide the body toward relaxation and breathing that is slow, deep, and deliberate

Stress Relaxation Exercise

While working in a residential setting, I enjoyed facilitating this activity for clients. Staff who came on the next shift would invariably comment on how quiet and relaxed the group appeared. Clients, I noticed, welcomed the opportunity to learn to relax. With staff encouraging them to take a time-out and do this stress relaxation exercise, clients became empowered with one more tool for self-help. I have also used this technique at my crisis intervention trainings for an end of the day treat.

The goal of the exercise is to facilitate slow, deep respirations. The brain will welcome the additional oxygen and, as a result, the body will relax and become invigorated. I have guided many different groups of people through this exercise, and it is not unusual for some to actually fall asleep while participating.

To begin, find your baseline heart rate. Check your pulse by placing your fingertips on the carotid artery, right below the joint connecting the jaw to the skull. Open and close your mouth to find the hinge and then move your fingers downward toward your throat until you feel the pulse. Time your pulse for ten seconds and multiply by six.

13 x 6 = 78 beats per minute.

Setting the Pace

Begin the exercise by inhaling slowly to a count of four. Think to yourself or have someone else say out loud:

"One, one-thousand; two, one-thousand; three, one-thousand; four, one-thousand"

Think about filling your stomach area or lower lungs first. Hold your breath in for a three second count:

"One, one-thousand; two, one-thousand; three, one-thousand."

Exhale slowly to a count of four.

"One, one-thousand; two, one-thousand; three, one-thousand; four, one-thousand."

Do this three times, then increase to a five count, hold for a four count, and exhale to a five count. After ten cycles, check your pulse at the carotid artery again. When done correctly, such an exercise can dramatically reduce your respiration and heart rate. At first you may not notice a drop in your pulse rate. If this is a new concept, it may take time to teach the body to relax. You can try doing more than ten cycles. Remember that you might want to increase the count as you go along, which helps to further slow your breathing. Slow deep breaths ensure the brain is receiving plenty of oxygen.

Breathing exercises are great for reducing the anxiety associated with fear or uncertainty. With practice you can use this stress relaxation exercise before, during, and after an intervention.

I like to begin and end each Aikido class with a breathing exercise. Each of us leads very busy lives, and after a full day, it feels right to sit quietly at the beginning of class and reflect on the simple act of breathing. During class, I constantly remind students to breathe, especially when I notice that their bodies look stiff or their faces look tightly held, grimacing. As students breathe, their shoulders drop and their faces relax. At the end of every class, we purposely focus our breathing once more to slow ourselves down after an active workout.

We have a weekly children's class for students between five and eleven years of age. Some of the six- and seven-year-olds have been attending for two years. After class, they stay in the gym and play together while their parents practice in the adult class. The room, as you can imagine, becomes filled with giggles. It can get downright loud, and sometimes we have to ask the children to lower their voices. It's interesting that at the end of the adult class, while we are doing our breathing exercise, the children hush each other and grow silent. It is as if their bodies are swept away by the power of purposeful breathing, as if the concerted breath of the adults is shared by everyone in the room.

Power of Suggestion

Medical personnel administer oxygen when a person is having difficulty breathing in order to sustain their organs and brain. As an intervener, when you don't have oxygen available, you still have the power of suggestion. The breathing-relaxation technique can be used in conjunction with oxygen and emergency medical resuscitation, but it is not meant to replace these techniques.

In sixteen years as an EMT, I have often been amazed by the visible relief of patients in trauma when I suggest, "Think about your breathing." I can almost read their thoughts as their faces change from grimace to "Oh, yeah. I can do that." When a person is frightened, breathing is a tangible act and a wonderfully grounding task to focus on. When confronted by pain, fear, or an overwhelming obstacle, it is comforting to know that we can still control our breath.

Suggesting slower breaths or providing a count: "breathe in, one, two, three, four. Hold it, one, two, three. Breathe out, one, two, three, four," has an immediate impact on a person's well-being. Inadequate ventilation makes people feel dizzy, listless, and frightened. As soon as the level of oxygen is increased, the body is able to relax and a renewed sense of well-being results. The following example illustrates.

Breathing with a Patient

The station wagon had rolled over the guardrail on the side of the highway. Everyone was still in the car except for the driver, who had been thrown about twenty five yards away against a cyclone fence. She had not been wearing a seat belt.

She lay face down, motionless. An off-duty state trooper had dug out the soil around her face so she could breathe. He and I felt desperate, unable to help her without any medical supplies except for my woolen blanket for shock. She had a weak pulse and shallow breathing. I kept asking her to stay with us and listen to her breathing. Coaxing, I repeated "Breathe easy. That's good," over and over. With the sirens wailing in the distance, she started to moan. She began to move as if reaching up. I had realized that she was the mother of the two kids still in the car. I said, "The girls are safe. They still need you." And then her body relaxed. The three of us were breathing in unison as the stretcher was brought down the embankment.

This woman had been expending all her energy moaning and trying to move. Reducing her anxiety and giving her direction in the form of a focus on breathing helped her relax and provided her brain with desperately needed oxygen. At the same time, I reminded the woman that her daughters were dependent upon her. I didn't want her to relax so completely that she might give up the fight for her life. Remember that setting a rhythm to follow, such as a count, or repeating "Breathe" should follow the initial suggestion to breathe.

If a Technique Works, Pass It On

I never hide my strategy for de-escalating a crisis. People don't like feeling that they are being manipulated and will say so. "I know what you are doing. You can't make me stop if I don't want to!" I actually prefer knowing that the person with whom I am intervening is present enough to notice the techniques I am using. I interpret obstinate responses, like the one above, to mean that they are hearing part of what I am saying or at least paying attention to me. They may not understand the entire motive behind my actions, but I am not being ignored. My reply would be, "It's good that you see what I am doing. I need your attention and help to work this out." People in distress need calm, skilled guidance to gain self-control. In time, they themselves may use the same techniques with another client, friend, or family member.

When a colleague of mine was visiting from out of state, I gave her driving directions and put up a sign on the telephone pole near my house that I knew she couldn't miss. On an old piece of wood with a green magic marker, I wrote the word, "Breathe."

At the time, I lived on the Wendell Town Common, a classic New England setting with century-old, white meeting halls, a one-room library, a bandstand, and surrounding homes. She told me with a laugh as she got out of her car that she knew I was close by when she saw the sign. My friend knew about my association with breathing as a conflict management technique.

I left the sign up, and it was there for over a year. From time to time, I would overhear townspeople talk about the sign. "You know, each time I drive by that 'Breathe' sign, I just take in a deep breath. It's a good reminder."

In 1995, the *Boston Globe Magazine* had a feature article called "A Town Like Wendell." To my surprise, in the center of the article was a small paragraph stating, "On the edge of the common, tacked to a pole at the corner of Locke's Hill and Center Road, is a hand-painted sign that reads, simply, 'Breathe.'"

The impact of the unplanned experiment of the 'Breathe' sign deepened my conviction in the value of simple and practical interventions. Redirecting conflict means using tools that will empower those in crisis to regain self-control. Whether intervening during a conflict or a medical emergency, the influence of breath has never failed to impress me. For the intervener, in the heat of the moment, remembering to breathe or helping others breathe is no small task. Exhaling is the first essential step toward maintaining a normal rate of respiration. Then, the intervener can guide others in normalizing their breathing as a means of restoring self-control.

Breathing awareness is a powerful tool for effective intervention and another way of creating a safe scene.

Cause No Harm

When asked how Aikido differs from other martial arts, I bow out of trying to make comparisons. I truly only know about Aikido, and even with this martial art after years of practice, I feel like a beginner. Aikido, like any art form, develops ever-growing depth of knowledge and wisdom through practice.

I like to speak of Aikido's attraction for me. The physical movements within the practice of this martial art are both beautiful to watch and a joy to experience and perform. Learning to move with an inner sense of calm and balance is one of the many rewards. Beyond physical elements of Aikido is the philosophy, at its best summed up as to cause no harm.

There are people who, if left to their own devices, would hurt others or themselves. Aikido provides the resources for safely and humanely containing a person who is a danger. I wish that there was never a need to physically restrain a person, but the day has not yet arrived. Therefore, I seek constantly to review how to help people who are dangerous to themselves or others—and to do so with the underlying intention of causing no harm.

One of my roles as a consultant in the field of conflict management is to review use of force policies. When you see the word use of force, it may conjure up images of men in white putting a straitjacket on a person. Perhaps it rekindles memories of the 1991 incident of Los Angles police officers who were caught in the act of brutally beating Rodney King Jr., after he was pulled over for a traffic violation. "Yuck," you may be thinking, "I don't want to read about manhandling a person," or you might still be scratching you head trying to figure out what exactly is the use of force.

Use of Force Defined

Use of force as defined in the context of conflict management is the use of a hands-on technique. Hands-on consists of any and all physical contact, such as holding a person's wrist or placing a hand on another person's arm in order to guide and escort.

The sectors of our society that use some form of physical force as part of their conflict management model are wide-ranging and diverse. The following are just a few: the military, law enforcement, education, residential treatment settings, parents and guardians, and hospitals. There is a great difference between the use of force in law enforcement and physical interventions in educational settings. Despite the different types of physical force used at one site versus another, there is a general standard denoting when force should be used.

This chapter will explore the use of physical intervention as a conflict management tool and the need for a universal code of conduct for the use of force. For workers who are expected to use force as part of their job duties, this chapter will be especially helpful. Although use of force is a fairly clinical term, think twice before skipping over this chapter. Everyone, whether parent or professional intervener, family member or patient, is impacted by the use of force in our society.

I have found that most people would prefer to either completely ignore the topic of use of force or talk about the use of force behind closed doors. The risk of injury for all parties involved in the application of the use of force contributes to reluctance about discussing it. The Pulitzer Prize-winning five-part series in the *Hartford Courant* newspaper in 1998 called "Deadly Restraint" sent a shiver of concern for human service providers across the nation. The series began with the heading, "Hundreds of the nation's most vulnerable have been killed by the system intended to care for them." One particular restraint technique, crossing a person's arms across his or her chest and pinning him or her in this position face down upon the floor, was found to be a potentially deadly hold, particularly for children. The Hartford Courant findings from a fifty state survey "confirmed 142 deaths during or shortly after restraint or seclusion in the past decade."

The discussion on the need to use force and what is deemed as a reasonable amount of force continues to evolve. Use of force policies can appear vague from the outset. There are so many "what if's" involved in real life conflicts, such as, "What if my facility says that I can't use force, but I walk into a room and find a person being beaten up pretty badly? What do I do then? Do I just call the police and watch that person being killed?" or "If I see a child in my classroom going to attack another student with a sharp pencil, can I intervene?"

To both queries the answer is to use common sense. Many work sites do not authorize employees to use force. Such sites can not justify having a worker like a teacher leave a group of students unsupervised while he or she tries to break up a fight between two people. To do so would put not only the teacher but also the rest of the students at risk of harm. With that said, there will continue to be challenges to rules governing the use of force, such as the teacher who stops a student from stabbing another child with a pencil. Despite the fact that grabbing the student's hand to prevent the stabbing appears to be an obvious course of action, the teacher may nevertheless be asked to file a report or, worse, face a lawsuit. We live in a very litigious time. Even when you are authorized to use *think* force, you may still be investigated to see if you exhausted all your resources before choosing to intervene physically.

Use of Force Complicates Conflict Management

Bear in mind an important goal: To cause no harm. Your intention when entering a scene that has escalated to the point where physical management is necessary will govern the techniques you choose. A person whose only recourse is to meet violence with greater violence will indeed complicate matters by using excessive force. If you are the intervener who must use force, don't allow a conflict to become complicated. Maintain self-control and keep your goals in order.

When Is the Use of Force Permissible?

The most widely used standard permitting the use of force during conflict management is stated as follows: It is permissible to use force when a person is a danger to self or others.

Attempting to commit suicide is an example of endangering one's own life. A police officer who reaches for a person trying to jump from a bridge exemplifies a permissible use of force.

School administrators and teachers are the guardians of the student body. A student may be considered at risk if she leaves a classroom or exits the building without supervision. The following vignette examines authorized use of force in a classroom setting.

A Student at Risk

Mr. Stine had noticed that Billy was not working on his assignment with the rest of the third graders in his special needs classroom. Mr. Stine had wanted to go over and help Billy out, but the teacher's assistant had called in sick that morning, and Mr. Stine was overwhelmed. "I'll be with you in a minute, Billy, to help you out, okay?" Mr. Stine called out to the daydreaming boy across the room. When Billy didn't acknowledge him, Mr. Stine knew that the boy's behavior would only get worse. When he looked up again, Billy had moved to the door and was starting to leave the room.

"Billy, wait a minute." Mr. Stine called. But Billy was already out the door and into the hallway.

Behavior of this type happens every day at schools across the nation. For the most part, educators are able to reason with a student who leaves a classroom or a school building. Talking is and should always be the first choice, but a third grader's safety is considered at risk when he leaves a classroom or school building without permission. Depending upon staffing availability, training, and the school district's use of force policy and protocol, Mr. Stine could very well be within his rights as a teacher to stop Billy physically.

How could Billy be physically stopped in a safe manner?

Grabbing Billy by the wrist as his mother might do when leading him across a busy intersection is not considered to be a safe physical management hold. Crisis intervention training programs that specialize in physical management techniques teach holds that are designed to minimize the risk of injury to both the person being held and the intervener. Protecting interveners from jabbing elbows and keeping the person's limbs close to his or her sides decreases the likelihood of injury for all parties involved during a physical management intervention.

Although leading Billy by the wrist may work, it is not considered a safe hold because his elbow is not secured from swinging out and hitting the intervener. Instead, the teacher can direct Billy by applying a soft escort. This particular hold is taught in the Response Crisis Intervention Model. Application of this technique involves placement of the intervener's hand above a student's elbow and below his or her shoulder. The intervener's other hand is lightly held over the student's elbow. Only staff who have received training in the correct application of the Soft escort are authorized to use the hold.

If you have read this far, I must have your attention, but you may still be thinking, "Holy smokes. If I were Billy's parent I would just grab his wrist." Perhaps you would, especially if that type of grab is all you know. Professionals, though, are expected to use hands-on techniques that reduce the risk of injury. If there are other options available, you can be sure that teachers of crisis intervention trainings will seek out the least injurious technique for all parties. With that said, however, parents do have more leeway to use force on their own children. I hold hope that parents and guardians are actively seeking disciplinary options that, in the end, cause no mental or physical harm to their children.

Other Options besides Using Force to Manage Billy

There is always an opportunity to exercise less invasive interventions. An alternative to using force in this student's case is to assign a staff member to follow Billy from a distance. Meanwhile, a parent / guardian and the police should be notified if he leaves the building. Educators have often discussed such scenarios during my seminars and all agree that a student will typically act as if she is leaving the grounds but instead will hide behind a swing set or a tree while she cools down her temper. Once done, she will return to the classroom and willingly participate.

The Goal of Using Force

Although the use of force may be authorized in Billy's case, there are alternatives to exercising its use. Notifying parents and watching Billy from a distance does take time away from educators who are already overburdened with responsibilities. Yet, with or without the use of force, this intervention is going to take time. If Billy is physically stopped from leaving school grounds, he is likely to become combative and will need a supervised cooling-down time. Supervision takes time, of course.

Billy and the interveners are equally at risk if the decision is to use "hands-on." Bumps and bruises can be expected even when state-of-the-art physical management techniques are used. And what about the other students, teachers, or visitors who may see Billy being physically forced to comply? Bearing witness to a physical intervention is not a pleasant experience. In fact, it can have a terrorizing impact that is long-lasting. Not only will Billy need to be attended to once the initial intervention is over, but all who witness the intervention should be debriefed and assessed to make sure that they feel safe and not fearful of being harmed themselves.

Mr. Stine had felt that the scene was likely to escalate, but he was working solo, and this complicated matters. Leaving one student to attend to another may not only have failed to keep Billy in the classroom, but it may have caused a chain reaction of events: "What about me, Mr. Stine?" "No, over here; Billy gets all the attention." "I thought you were going to help me!"

When you are responsible for a group of people, you have to weigh in how your choice will impact not only the individual, but the entire group. Mr. Stine may have been able to leave the student he was attending to in order to go directly to Billy when he first noticed his nonparticipation. It would depend upon the teacher's relationship with his students and the norms he has set in delegating others to act in a reasonable fashion when peers are having a hard time. In this case, Mr. Stine actually called attention to Billy's behavior, a move that could have waited until he was able to dedicate more time to Billy.

Mr. Stine decided to call the vice-principal's office and inform the secretary of Billy's departure. She in turn notified the vice-principal who then walked up the hallway and met Billy walking toward the main office. Billy did not reply to the vice-principal's greeting but did, however, walk with the vice-principal to the main office. Once in the office, Billy took a seat. The vice-principal kept a watchful eye on the boy and, after five minutes of sitting, Billy was able to move into the vice-principal's office and discuss his behavior in Mr. Stine's class. Physical force was avoided in Billy's case because he did not run from the vice-principal's care and was able to regain a sense of self-control, demonstrated by his willingness to sit quietly in the vice-principal's office.

In the Goal-Oriented Intervention Model, the purpose of using force is to sustain and maintain safety for both the agitated party and those involved who might be targeted and in harm's way. When deciding to use force to control another person's actions, the intervener should always be acting with the intention to cause no harm.

Goal-Oriented Intervention Model

CONFLICT MANAGEMENT GOAL	⟶	*Help Those in Conflict Regain a Sense of Self-control*
		↓
PHYSICAL MANAGEMENT GOAL	⟶	*Cause No Harm*

The goal of causing no harm can be achieved when interveners are trained in hands-on techniques for physically managing conflict. Parents or professional interveners who lack physical management skills and attempt to use force risk their own safety and that of others. Instead of utilizing hands-on techniques that reduce the risk of injury, unskilled interveners rely on physical techniques that are often combative and destructive.

The Unskilled Use of Force and a Feeling of Hopelessness
The fight-or-flight response to conflict can prompt you to flee a scene, respond verbally, or engage in hand-to-hand combat in an attempt to control an incident. The ability to manage a conflict effectively is virtually nil if one's self-control is compromised. Feelings of hopelessness, fear of injury, and fear of loss of self-control all ignite an emotional response. Such a response coupled with the unskilled use of force increases the likelihood of inflicting harm. Interveners may then resort to street fighting maneuvers, military combat moves, or frantic flailing at anyone who comes into their grasp.

There are many dangerous "techniques" used by unskilled interveners: choke holds, strikes and kicks to the head or abdomen, bear hugs that compromise another's oxygen supply, and shoving, slapping, and poking that deliver substantial, if not life threatening injuries.

The following vignette illustrates a parental use of force that is ill-suited, life-threatening, and reactionary.

A Father's Misuse of Force

Nick Carson heard banging on the ceiling above his head and knew that his two teenage boys were probably fighting again. They had been at each other's throats all day, and Nick was tired of it all. He walked upstairs and opened their bedroom door. Nick walked into the boys' room without a pause and hit the boy closest to him on the side of head with a strong, right-handed punch. Alex dropped to the floor like a dead weight and didn't get up. "You want some too, Benny?" shouted Nick. Benny had backed off instantly when he saw his father punch Alex. "Get up, Alex. I want this room cleaned up. It looks like a pig sty." Alex was laid out on the floor. His teeth were clenched and his body was rigid.

When Nick saw the expression on Alex's face, he knew instantly there was something wrong with his son. "Oh, Lord, what have I done?" cried the father.

Physical force should not be used as a punitive measure during conflict management. Addressing consequences is part of the crisis-conflict resolution stage. This is not to say that the father should punch his son on the side of the head once he has secured scene safety. Nick should not punch Alex or Benny in anger or at all. Assaultive behavior is never productive and typically causes serious physical and mental harm to the recipient.

Nick didn't even try to distract his sons or command them to stop fighting. If a family's level of communication is so stressed that two sons ignore their own father's demands, the police should be called. Taking matters into one's own hands under such circumstances will only serve to further escalate the conflict. Perhaps, on occasion, Nick would be physically able to stop his sons from fighting. How many times can a parent intercede in this manner without also putting herself at risk and causing physical harm to her child? Addressing consequences when you are in control of your emotions and not acting with blind rage is a sound practice and protects everyone involved from undue harm.

Let's give Nick another chance to manage his sons' fight. This time, he won't use force.

Nick heard banging on the ceiling above his head and knew that his two teenage boys were probably fighting again. They had been at each other's throats all day, and Nick was tired of it all. He walked upstairs and opened their bedroom door and stood for a moment. Alex had his arm wrapped around Benny's head. "Say you're sorry or I won't let go." Benny was bent over and squealing, "No way."

In a loud and steady voice the father said, "Alex. Let Benny go." Nick then took two steps forward into the boys' room. Alex reluctantly shoved Benny away from him. "Benny, go downstairs and wait for me in the living room, son." Benny left the room without looking back.

With the two boys separated, the target of their immediate anger was removed. The father was in a better position to mediate the dispute with each boy separately. Initially pausing at the door and taking his time to assess the scene not only gave Nick Carson time to compose himself, but it also made his intervention stand out. If he had quickly moved into the room demanding Alex to let go, his son may not have immediately noticed him. Quiet composure in the midst of chaos is an effective technique that catches the attention of those in conflict.

Hands-off Policies and their Effect on Workers

Workers who must follow a hands-off policy of their work site often feel frustrated or helpless. "Are we expected to just stand there and watch as another person is being beaten up? I just couldn't do that. I would have to try to stop the fight!"

said Mark, a direct care staff at an emergency shelter for juveniles. For Mark, compromising his compassion goes against the very reason he entered the human service field. Yet, injuries are likely when you fail to follow a work site protocol. If there is an inadequate staff-to-client ratio, one staff person intervening puts the rest of his charges at risk if the worker is injured.

Work sites that have a hands-off policy, meaning that employees are not to use physical force when intervening, rely instead on the local police to assist. Relinquishing authority to the police can create conflicts for the requesting agency, however. Once the police are involved, jurisdiction over the scene is in control of the police, possibly compounding workers' initial feelings of hopelessness in making the call.

In a threatening situation, interveners may take a defensive posture to convey physical readiness. However, when you become confident with the dynamics of speaking to an agitated person, you are more inclined to use verbal skills first to de-escalate a hostile incident.

Professionals who work at sites that serve aggressive populations should be provided with ongoing training in verbal intervention. Policies and procedures regarding the management of aggressive behavior should be reviewed with employees to ensure that appropriate emergency protocols will be followed if a violent scene erupts.

Job Descriptions in Relation to Use of Force

For work sites that do authorize use of force, clarification is essential as to when and to what degree an employee is expected to intervene physically. In facilities serving a potentially aggressive population, job descriptions will often include statements like the following:

"Workers may be required to do physical restraints."

This statement gets right to the point. Other descriptions are not as straightforward.

"Workers are responsible for the security and well-being of the [clients, students, patients]."

Clarification on the particulars of one's job duties as they pertain to hands-on interventions should be found in the agency's use of force policy.

Use of Force Policy

How far do you go in assuring the welfare of another person? If a person is being assaulted by another, should the police be called or should workers physically intervene? A use of force policy describes when force, meaning a physical hands-on intervention, can and cannot be used.

A use of force policy might have the following clauses defining when the welfare of a person is at risk and when force can be used.

Use of force can be invoked only when:
- a person is a danger to self or others
- a person will not follow a directive

Some policies will also authorize workers to use force:
- in self defense
- to prevent people from inflicting major property damage.

Along with the job description, the use of force policy tells workers what their duties are in terms of "providing for the safety and well being of the [clients, students, patients]" by defining the following:
- type of force with clearly defined techniques
- degree of force or amount of force to be used
- amount of time force should be applied
- medical follow-up

Hands-on Techniques

Hands-on interventions can vary from soft escorts to full immobilization. The escort might involve simply placing a hand on an agitated person's arm between the elbow and the shoulder. Workers who are responsible for the security and well-being of extremely violent and assaultive people are usually provided training in full immobilization. A full immobilization would be used when, while being restrained, a person tries to injure himself or others by head butting, kicking, scratching, and biting.

The use of force policy should clearly state which techniques are authorized to be used by workers.

For example:

Workers can only use the techniques that are specifically taught during the on-site crisis intervention training program. These include the following, as taught during the on-site crisis intervention training:

- soft escort
- underarm escort
- holding technique

Appropriate Degree of Force

Workers can use "the degree of force necessary to gain control." This critical phrase is used in many use of force documents. Interpretation of this phrase varies, but for the most part, employees are expected to use common sense. If a person calls you a derogatory name and you respond by putting her in a restraint, it would be considered excessive force. Verbal intervention would have been a more appropriate response.

Abuse of Force in the Classroom Setting

Gary and Martha worked as teacher assistants at an elementary school. They were both trained crisis interveners and were the first ones called when a child became disruptive.

Peter, an eleven-year-old student, refused to participate in the lesson being taught by his teacher. He pushed over his chair, and the other children backed away. His teacher called the main office. The secretary, in turn, called Gary and Martha, who were both temporarily relieved of their duties. When Gary and Martha asked Peter to come with them into the hallway, Peter kicked at Gary and hit him directly in the shin.

When Martha asked Gary if he was okay, Gary, said, "Just fine. Let's go!" while moving toward Peter. Gary put his hands on Peter, and Martha followed her coworker. While Peter was being held, he was yelling "You're hurting me! Let go!"

Martha saw that Gary's knuckles were turning white while gripping Peter's wrist. "Loosen up, Gary," said Martha. Gary ignored his coworker and held on tighter. "Gary!" demanded Martha, *"Loosen up now!"*

Gary was unable to control his impulse of wanting to get even with Peter for kicking him. His tightening grip, white knuckles, and unwillingness to listen to Martha indicated that Gary was unable to control his emotions.

Interventions like Gary's demonstrate the need for maintaining professionalism and self-control. Getting kicked or spit at are some of the indignities that staff sometimes experience in work environments that serve potentially volatile population. Learning how to control the impulse to react during an intervention should be part of every crisis intervention training.

Sometimes, despite impulse control, the best option is to leave the intervention and let another worker who is not emotionally tied to the incident take over. When Gary was kicked, he should have backed away from the scene and composed himself. If he could not let go of his anger toward Peter for kicking him in the shin, Gary should have excused himself and had someone else like the principal step in and take over his role as intervener. When a worker has become emotionally reactive, he should leave the scene. A common code used by coworkers to give space to another is, "You have a phone call," a euphemistic way of saying take a time-out.

Martha could have tried to help her team member by saying to Gary when he first got hit, "Hold up. Let's both take a deep breath with Peter and try this over again." Such a statement includes the person in crisis and would reset the mood for an intervention that has started off on the wrong foot. Another option might have been to remove Peter's classmates to another room, a viable option used by many schools. With the removal of spectators, an angry person will be better able to focus on the situation at hand without feeling the need to perform in front of peers.

Amount of Time Hands-on Can Be Used

The use of force policy should contain a statement describing the length of time that hands-on can be used. For instance, the policy might state that a person can be restrained for up to five minutes, at which time a supervisor has to provide authorization for hands-on to continue. Without such guidelines, a person could theoretically be restrained indefinitely.

Assessing a person's readiness to be released from a restraint is a procedure that should be taught to workers during a crisis intervention training. Regaining a normal breathing pattern, verbally acknowledging those who are intervening, and agreeing to parameters of the release are three indicators used to determine a person's readiness to be released.

Medical Follow-Up

Although many treatment facilities or schools are not mandated to provide medical follow-up after a restraint, such reviews promote quality of care for both the person who was held and the intervener. At times, people do get injured during physical interventions. Medical review helps to determine if the application of a restraint was done properly or if the physical hold being applied is contributing to a particular injury. The *Hartford Courant's* series brings to light a particular hold that was responsible for a number of deaths throughout the United States. The facedown floor hold, with a person's arms held under his or her own body, has been banned by many states. Unfortunately, it took a journalistic exposé to bring to light a process that should have been reviewed in-house by each facility using force as part of their conflict management model.

When a person requires full immobilization, a medical examination should be done after the holding period. Using the local hospital or having a nurse on call is an option for agencies who wish to incorporate a medical follow-up into their use of force policy. Employees should be taught how to document an incident, and they should understand who reviews the form—and how.

Gray Areas with Use of Force Policies

The following examples illustrate some of the most common queries into use of force policies. For professional interveners, it is advisable to review questions during in-service trainings in order to clarify misconceptions on the use of force.

Use of Force: Destruction of Property—The Broken Pencil

Nancy Shelborn was a teacher at a residential treatment center for adolescents. Her agency's use of force policy specified that staff had the right to use force if one of the following existed:

- the student was in danger of harming herself or others
- the student did not follow a directive
- the student was destroying property

During Ms. Shelborn's Wednesday morning class with a group of girls, she noticed that Tracy Adams was whispering to another girl and pointing at Patty Fisch. Ms. Shelborn said, "Tracy, is there something going on that you would like to share with the rest of us?"

Tracy replied, "That bitch there has my shirt, and staff let her get away with it. She's got to pay her dues."

Ms. Shelborn stepped up to Tracy's desk and said, "You get once consequence for swearing. For threatening another student—"

Tracy cut her off: "Yeah, and what do I get for breaking this pencil? A trip to Disney World?" The rest of the class exploded with laughter when Tracy defiantly broke the pencil in half.

Had Ms. Shelborn found herself in a situation that justified the use of force? Although the policy said she had the right to use force if there was destruction to property, did breaking a pencil merit the use of force? Had Ms. Shelborn fully exhausted her verbal skills? Was this destruction to property a threat to others or herself? All of these questions should come to mind whenever an intervener is confronted with a situation that is potentially volatile. Ms. Shelborn could certainly make a convincing argument for needing to use force by stating that the student was inciting the class and was therefore a danger to herself and others. Resorting to a use of force, though, should only be done after an intervener has exhausted all possible alternatives for managing a scene. Conflict management does not consist solely of knowing what to say to a person; it also requires an understanding of how you portray and project your position of authority. Let's review how Ms. Shelborn provoked a potentially manageable situation into a conflict.

Ms. Shelborn's first intervention pushed Tracy into a position where she had to respond in a fashion so as not to "lose face" in front of her peers. Tracy was doing the right thing by telling the teacher exactly why she was upset. She could have lied and said, "Nothing," or she could have or made up a story, such as, "Oh, we were just talking about the movie last night." Instead of forming an alliance with the student based upon her truthfulness, Ms. Shelborn boxed Tracy into a position where she had nothing left to lose by being defiant. The incident was blown out of proportion and perhaps even taught the student to lie next time instead of telling the truth.

The situation started as a manageable conflict, but through her own error, the teacher escalated the incident into a stand-off between herself and the student. Ms. Shelborn should continue to intervene verbally and avoid physical intervention at all costs. Breaking a pencil can indeed become a physical threat, in the same way that any implement held in one's hand can potentially be used as a weapon. Ms. Shelborn should have determined if this pencil was going to be a weapon or simply a theatrical prop used by the student.

Using the same scenario, let's give Ms. Shelborn another chance at working with Tracy.

During Nancy Shelborn's Wednesday morning class with a group of girls, she noticed that Tracy Adams was whispering to another girl and pointing at Patty Fisch. Ms. Shelborn said, "Tracy, is there something going on that you would like to share with the rest of us?"

Tracy replied "That bitch there has my shirt, and staff let her get away with it. She's got to pay her dues."

Ms. Shelborn stepped up to Tracy's desk and said, "Thanks for telling me that. You do have a lot going on."

The teacher turned to face the rest of the class. She knew that the other students had overheard this brief exchange. Patty, meanwhile, was looking forward at the blackboard in a stoic pose.

"All right, everyone," the teacher began. "Now I'm going to give Tracy some advice that you are welcome to listen to. I do not, however, expect any outbursts."

Ms. Shelborn turned to Tracy and said, "You are on the right track by speaking about a conflict. I am recommending that you continue to speak to a staff member back at your cottage, or you can stay to speak with me after class."

"Yeah, whatever," Tracy replied.

"'Whatever' is not how I see it. It's all about caring and making the right choices," said the teacher.

The teacher then walked over to Patty's desk and encouraged her also to stay after class.

Ms. Shelborn used the situation as a teaching moment in both of the preceding examples. She also set a boundary by telling the students what was acceptable behavior: no outbursts. This time, the use of force never became an issue. Working with Tracy is less time consuming than managing a scene that requires a use of force. Both the teacher and the students benefit from such interventions.

Use of Force: Major Property Damage—Erik's Fluorescent Bulb

The psychiatric hospital for men and women was an older building, and the state was in the process of securing money to build a new state-of-the-art facility. Too many tiles were missing from the floors, and the overhead lighting was less than adequate. Staff were constantly on alert for patients getting their hands on loose debris from the already dilapidated building.

Cheryl and John, who worked second shift, were both in the staff office finishing up paperwork. The other three workers were in the social room talking and playing cards with patients. It was seven o'clock in the evening, and everyone gathered as usual in the social room to wind down after a long day.

The use of force policy at the hospital stated that staff could use force to prevent patients from harming themselves or others.

Cheryl and John were first on the scene after they heard Erik, one of the patients, yelling out from the library. They found Erik standing in the middle of the reading room holding a four-foot long fluorescent bulb and shouting out, "All right, men. The enemy is in our sight!" Erik then kicked over a large oak table in the center of the room and hid behind it. Cheryl immediately called for additional assistance, and soon there were six hospital workers on the scene. John was talking to Erik from the hallway. Erik responded by shouting out, "Fire!" and throwing a ball of paper he had torn from a book.

The staffing team on hand decided to wait out Erik's behavior until he initiated a "peace treaty." The fluorescent bulb in Erik's hand presented too great a risk of danger for Erik and the staff, since toxic dust and glass fragments would be released if he broke the bulb. Meanwhile, one team member called the police to help assist if Erik did, indeed, decide to break the bulb. Erik appeared to be content behind his barricade in the library, since he was making no move to leave the room. The supervisor on duty hoped to avoid the risk of wrestling away a large fluorescent bulb from a psychotic patient.

Erik did break the bulb in half and started toward the door leading out of the library. The police arrived at the same time and stood at the entrance to the library. When Erik saw the two police officers in uniform, he immediately put down his weapon and walked compliantly out of the room.

Even when there is authorization to use force, it may still be in everyone's best interest to bring in police assistance. Intervening when a person is holding a knife or, in this case, a long glass lighting fixture that contains toxic chemicals requires sophisticated skills in physical intervention.

The police have a number of options available to them. Their decision about using force will be based upon whether they are being directly targeted, whether the person is targeting someone else, or whether the person is trying to inflict injury upon himself.

On-site security or police officers are often called to hospital emergency rooms in order to stand by in case a patient becomes disruptive. I have worked with officers who have moved in too quickly, thereby escalating a scene that might have been managed verbally. For instance, while working in an ER with a young man who had attempted suicide, it was my role to tell him that he was being involuntarily committed to a psychiatric hospital for further evaluation. I had met with the police officers when they first arrived. They were called in to act as back up in case the patient became volatile while I told him about the commitment proceedings. I had asked them to stand by while I spoke to the patient, but they made their presence known as soon as I approached the young man. Although the patient was not being combative as I spoke to him, he became loud and disrespectful toward us as the officers on duty moved toward him.

Relinquishing control of the scene to the police decreases the likelihood of harm to staff and patients. Maintaining an active dialogue with the local police department is a proactive measure for any facility that works with a volatile population, even if there is a use of force policy allowing staff to physically intervene.

Avoiding Physical Intervention

Everything was going smoothly on Wednesday morning as the buses were arriving at the middle school. Then bus Number 7 pulled onto school grounds. Jack Cann, the vice-principal, and Lee Wu, the teacher on duty that morning, immediately noticed bus Number 7 as it moved up to the front of the building. All the children on the bus looked as if they were standing. When the bus door opened, Mr. Cann stepped up to the door and looked to Frances Holmes, the driver, for an explanation. She immediately said, "Sam is yelling at another boy in the back of the bus. I think he is starting a fight."

If Sam and the other boy began fighting, should Mr. Cann have immediately intervened and tried to break up the fight?

Mr. Cann knew that safety was the first priority. His personal safety was not at risk. The scene on the bus, though, was definitely not safe, and he was responsible for the entire busload of children. The quickest way to make the majority of the children safe was to get them off the bus. Mr. Cann instructed Mr. Wu and Mrs. Holmes to quickly and quietly get the rest of the students off the bus. He then began to move to the back of the bus. Sam was yelling at another boy who was cornered in the farthest seat in the back. The other boy looked pleadingly at Mr. Cann.

Mr. Cann said, "Sam, it is time to get off the bus."

Sam replied, "I'm not leaving until he gives me my money." The bus had emptied, and Mr. Cann saw that Mr. Wu was standing outside the back door of the bus to provide assistance if necessary.

If Mr. Cann tried to move forcefully Sam off the bus, the risk of injury would be high in such closed quarters. In general, it is always best to allow an agitated person to move of his or her own accord. Mr. Cann decided that since Sam was acknowledging him, there was a chance for further dialogue.

The vice-principal sat in the seat in front of Sam and the other boy. "I want to help out, Sam," he said, "but this bus has to move out to pick up the kids going to the high school. How about stepping off the bus so you can tell me what's up?"

"I don't want to leave until he pays me back," said Sam.

"I hear that, but this bus has got to keep moving and we all have to get off," Mr. Cann said softly.

"Get another bus," yelled Sam.

"Sam, I'm here to help you," said Mr. Cann.

Slowly, Sam turned and made his way down the aisle of the bus.

At no time during this period did Mr. Cann begin asking Sam or the other boy what was going on. Instead, he took the target of Sam's anger away by directing the conversation to the need for the bus to keep moving. In this way, the three became allies in having to get off the bus together.

In closed quarters, like a school bus, it is best to continue to use verbal intervention and to avoid physical intervention. I have been in the "hot seat" like Mr. Cann. The only difference was that I was in a van full of eight adolescents, male and female, and the van was moving. My coworker was driving the fifteen-passenger van home from an off-grounds activity. A boy sitting in the back of the van started picking a fight with another boy. We were about fifteen minutes away from the secure facility, and it was up to me to go back and manage the scene.

I asked the other kids to move as far forward as possible, and they complied. Then I sat in the seat in front of the disruptive teen. I was well aware of the confined space and, thus, my potentially compromised safety. I engaged in a nonthreatening conversation with the young man. Every time he made a derogatory remark about someone in the van, including me, I listened but didn't challenge him. Instead I would say, "You have been doing so well in the program."

I was able to keep the teen distracted, seated, and engaged until the vehicle stopped. I had to keep my cool and stay on my guard, since my charge was threatening to assault me, "I am going to go off on you and you can't stop me in this van," he said. I chose to take his words as indicative of hopelessness, because his threats were random and apparently without any intent to effect change. I continued to implore him to hang in there. "You can keep it together. I know you can." I also knew that keeping the conversation steady was really the only choice. If the driver had to pull over and help me contain the teen, there would have been a risk of injury to all of us. My goal-oriented strategy worked and confirmed my opinion that choosing to use force may sometimes be a necessity, but more often than not verbally engaging with an angry party is a viable option.

Use of Force Policies as Safeguards for the Innocent

A use of force policy involves more than just the determination of when physical force should be authorized. It addresses the need to protect workers and those they serve or care for from the abuse of physical force. People are vulnerable to abuse by workers who take revenge on them for acting out and resisting.

"Slapping Charges Lead to Probation" read the headline of the October 21, 1996 Greenfield, Massachusetts, *The Recorder* newspaper. A nurses' aide had slapped a mildly retarded eighty-eight-year-old patient on the side of the head after the patient had punched the aide in the chest. This had occurred while the aide was moving the patient onto a geriatric chair.

Punishing a person is not a permissible use of force. If you are feeling vengeful, it is best to leave the intervention and let someone else take over. An intervener who is unable to respond in a professional manner should step away from the conflict rather than victimize a person whose actions have spun out of control.

Modeling Alternatives to Violence

The intervener is the leader of the scene, setting the pace for the rest of the incident. Even when there has been an altercation, the leader must assess total scene safety. Immediately going in and breaking up a fight is not always the best choice for an intervener or the group at large. In a home, classroom setting or any other site where force may be used, interveners are role models. They should display what they deem to be good choices for managing a conflicts.

When an intervener is talking softly to a student in crisis, giving specific instructions like "Come with me" and remaining calm, the message is clear to all onlookers: crisis intervention does not mean that the intervener has to accelerate to the same level of agitation as the person in crisis. The use of force policy provides the guidelines for physical intervention, but the direction that the intervention takes is still up to the intervener(s).

Summary: Viability of Universal Approach to Use of Force

Can there be a universal approach in the use of force? It turns out that our society is already moving in that direction. Parents like Nick Carson, for example, who use excessive force on their children, are being called to task and charged with child abuse. Despite the parental right to govern one's children, there is still a need for accountability about use of force.

Most people don't think that guidelines would be necessary to govern private use of force. Any one of the vignettes in this chapter could have been reworked as a parent-child scenario. While it is difficult enough for professional interveners to sustain a level of self-control when managing a conflict, emotions are particularly high when family members are involved. Irreconcilable mental and physical damage can occur to another person when force is used arbitrarily or in the heat of the moment, especially by a family member.

Preventing unintentional injuries necessitates keeping a goal in mind when deciding to use force. "To make the classroom scene safe, I will have to move Johnny out of the classroom or move his classmates away from Johnny" defines the purpose behind using force in order to establish scene safety. In one possible example, swatting Johnny on the side of the head or twisting his arm until he cries out in pain has nothing to do with making the scene safe. Only an unskilled intervener would rely on street fighting tactics to get Johnny's attention. Interveners trained on the limitations and risks of using force understand the need to restrain their emotions and use only safe physical management techniques. Specifically, an intervener trained in the use of force will use the safest, minimal force required to achieve the desired goal—safety—of the intervention.

A parent or guardian can use the same model. "To get Johnny to stop fighting with his brother, I will move him to his room or ask his brother to leave the living room," Johnny's mother might say to herself. Leaving the emotional impact of Johnny's behavior temporarily out of the picture reduces the risk of his mother's wanting to lash out uncontrollably at him. She has only one goal in mind now: to make the scene safe. Discussing the conflict between Johnny and his brother can wait until both boys have settled down and his mother has been able to sort through her own emotions to make a decision that is based upon sound reasoning, not a knee-jerk reaction.

As useful as it is for managing conflict among non-family members, the Goal-Oriented Model also lessens the likelihood of hurting those we love and hold closest to our hearts. This model provides a universal code of conduct that can be used by professional interveners and parents alike.

The Model Relies on the Messenger

'Tis the motive exalts the action.
'Tis the doing, not the deed.
—Margaret Junkin Preston

When I first started teaching crisis intervention courses, I thought every crisis-conflict needed a specific game plan. As I gained experience and skills, I hoped to get through most crises. For the most part, I did okay. Like many others who face the challenges of the day with the resources at hand and a little luck, I survived. I managed to work with people in perpetual crisis, and I taught crisis intervention trainings relying solely on skills.

After a while, mere survival was not enough. Burnout was right around the corner, and I knew that if I didn't start doing something differently, I was going to meet it head on.

Looking for new direction, I began to see a pattern in my conflict management style: I was integrating my skills as an emergency medical technician and crisis intervener. The first aid goal of stabilizing a patient became part of my conflict management style as securing personal safety and scene safety. I found that by using my own style of conflict management, the overall scene became safe and manageable. I also found that I was able to ally myself with the best interests of those involved, I became much more enthusiastic and burnout no longer loomed on the horizon.,

The Goal-Oriented Intervention Model is such a basic concept with its emphasis on safety that I wondered how it would be embraced. At many trainings when I first introduce the model, I am met with resistance. One group that comes to mind was participating in a Response Instructor Certification course held in May of 2001. The fourteen participants worked at adult acute care psychiatric hospitals in Pennsylvania. Many of them had more than ten years' experience. Their backgrounds were diverse: there were psychiatric aides, registered nurses, and psychologists. They were all seasoned crisis interveners, and some had created on-site models at their respective hospitals for managing potentially volatile patients.

On the second day of training, the group was clearly struggling with the concept of safety as the primary goal of crisis intervention. They had all been integrating the idea of resolution into their conflict management models. The Goal-Oriented Intervention Model was contrary to what they had been doing and seemed initially too simple a concept for many in the group.

Staying true to our model, we allowed participants to speak out, but we also avoided becoming targets of their anger. It was clear they were resentful of our presentation. While my co-instructor Erica Hypnarowski and I felt physically safe from harm, I also knew the situation was emotionally unsafe. During some heated and almost hostile exchanges, one person said she didn't want to stay for the rest of the training.

The eyes of the group focused on Erica and me as the participants waited for a confrontation. Instead, they got no reaction from us other than our calm demeanor and even breathing. Eventually, I dismissed the class for lunch.

Separating the group and giving them a time-out from the mounting emotions and information overload helped alleviate tension. Erica and I were able to meet one-on-one with the participants. The lunch break provided a needed respite from the conflict, and everyone stayed safe.

Resolution occurred on the fifth day when the group collaborated without my knowing it on a verse based on their experience during the training. The little poem is entitled "Just Breathe." It is lighthearted and touches on all the elements of the Goal-Oriented Model. "We didn't believe you shouldn't resolve the problems of patients while giving a pause . . .," the participants wrote. "You insisted we stop and not jump to resolution . . . . Safe and controlled is the way we should be . . . We need only to exhale."

I was and am deeply touched by the words of poem. It illustrates the struggle within the group to integrate a new approach with the age-old task of conflict management.

More importantly, it speaks well of a group of people who have committed their lives to serving those among us who are potentially violent and mentally ill.

These new trainers are successfully incorporating the Response Goal-Oriented Intervention Model at Allentown State Hospital and Danville State Hospital in Pennsylvania. The woman who wanted to leave the five-day training is now one of the lead trainers at her site.

The Goal-Oriented Model works to keep safety in the forefront of conflict management, but ultimately, the model depends upon the integrity of the person utilizing it during each intervention.

Before I adopted the Goal-Oriented Model, I too struggled with changing my own approach to conflict management. Aikido has helped me to clarify my thoughts on the matter. As a practice, Aikido does not teach how to physically overpower another person. Rather, it provides a lesson in ego management. Aikido cannot be practiced alone; there is an interdependent relationship between training partners. In order for one

Aikidoist to succeed, all Aikidoists must succeed. At my own dojo, the place where I practice and teach Aikido, I count on my students to excel so that I may benefit from their success as they begin to test me.

I believe that we are all mutually dependent in the challenge of making our world a safer place. Helping people in conflict learn how to regain self-control and well-being is a worthy goal. By helping to restore personal safety and scene safety, the intervener can feel safe from harm, as can other participants in the conflict.

There will always be simple quarrels as well as extremely volatile confrontations, but it is not the potential chaos itself that I fear. Instead, I fear how easy it is to lose yourself in its midst. Choosing to bring order from chaos instead of allowing chaos to overcome you begins by simply pausing and exhaling—"Ahhh." Order has arrived.

Acknowledgments

There have been countless voices through the years that have helped shape me as a person and thus this book. Foremost, I thank all who have participated in the Response Program for your courage to try new ideas, to role-play, and to share triumphs and tribulations.

I am indebted to Laura Botkin who believed in this work and took on the task of editing the first drafts. I would also like to thank Elizabeth Yoakum for incomparable graphic design, Tom Hurlbut for expert photography, and Jane Gagliardi for wise editing. A special thanks to editor Marcia Gagliardi for helping to make this a better book and to Carolyn E. Donadio for her vision of an organization's potential to be compassionate.

I am grateful to family and friends who understood my absence and knew when to demand my presence while I was writing this book. My parents, Alexander and Ellen Pastick, have provided me with loving support and ideal role models. Lydia Elison always arrived at the perfect time to whisk me away for a three-hour walk. Amy, Tim, and Ella Bernard always had open hearts and arms

To the members of Wendell Aikido and the Aikido community at large "Domo arigato gozaimashita."

About the Author

Alexandria A. Windcaller, M. H. S. A., is a conflict management specialist. She is the founder and director of Response Training Programs, a staff development consulting firm providing conflict management and debriefing programs to public schools, juvenile treatment facilities, acute care psychiatric hospitals, corrections, law enforcement, and military personnel. She was a certified emergency medical technician for sixteen years. She authors a column for *Aikido Today Magazine* called "Off the Mat" and is the chief instructor at Wendell Aikido, a martial arts dojo, in Wendell, Massachusetts .